When Hurt Won't Stop
Keys to Healing Relationship Pain

By Debra George

With Foreword by Jesse & Cathy Duplantis

Scripture quotations herein are taken from The Amplified Bible, Old Testament, copyright © 1965, 1987 by the Zondervan Corporation and The Amplified New Testament copyright © 1958, 1987 by The Lockman Foundation. Use by permission. All rights reserved.

Scripture quotations herein are taken from the Holy Bible, King James Version, Cambridge, 1769.

Scripture quotations herein are taken from The New King James Bible, Thomas Nelson Publishers, Nashville, copyright © 1982. Used by permission. All rights reserved.

When Hurt Won't Stop
Keys to Healing Relationship Pain
ISBN – 1-9815-9014-5
ISBN 13 – 978-1-9815-9014-8

For more information about Debra George, visit www.debrageorge.org.
Contact Info: debrageorgeministries@gmail.com

Cover Art: Ashlee Wilsher

All rights reserved under International Copyright Law. Contents and/or cover may not be reproduced in whole or in part in any form without the express written consent of Debra George Ministries.

Foreword

Debra George is a victorious powerhouse for God and a terror to the devil! In the many years that we have known Debra, we have found her to be so passionate about her calling as a soul winner that it's actually contagious! In seminars around the world, her anointed messages help people of all ages and backgrounds to reach their God-given potential.

In her book, **When Hurt Won't Stop**, Debra shares her own journey out of the pain of a broken relationship and into a life of joy and purpose. Instead of seeing yourself as a victim, a survivor, or failure in life, her book will inspire you to hold your head up and see the bright future that God has just for you. You can go all the way with God, no matter what life may throw at you!

Jesse & Cathy Duplantis
Jesse Duplantis Ministries

What Others Have to Say About the Book....

The night baby sister (sister-in-law) fell into our arms, weeping and broken, is forever etched into our memories – not because of the weeping and brokenness we experienced as Debra poured her heart out – but because of her answer to a question I asked her. "Debra, if your husband never returns; if nothing works out like you know it should; if God never answers another prayer; if all of your dreams and desires lay shattered before you, what will you do?" Her answer was simply this, "I will keep on serving Jesus!" From 2AM, until the dawning of the day, was Debra's darkest hour. Little did she know, her one decision created the dawning of a new life. Ephesians 6:13 (AMP) says, "...having done all the crises demands, stand firmly in your place."

Pastor Richard Ford
Family Worship Center

What can I say about baby sister? Except, she was thrown into a pit, but she didn't stay there. Thrown into a furnace, but she didn't stay there. Faced with the biggest Goliath of her life, but came out fighting with a slingshot and a stone and took the Word of God and overcame every obstacle that the enemy threw at her. You're a champion of God and a trophy in the body of Christ. 2 Corinthians 2:14 says, "But thanks be to God who in Christ always leads us in triumph as trophies of Christ's victory and through us spreads and makes evident the fragrance of the knowledge of God everywhere." I'm so glad I had the privilege to lead you to Jesus in my living room, many years ago. I love you and I am proud of you!

Pastor Tena Ford
Family Worship Center

Inside the book, **When Hurt Won't Stop**, Debra shares powerful and insightful truths that will help you let go of your painful past and move forward into your God-given destiny. Debra's transparency and openness, in sharing her journey, is refreshing! I have known Debra since 1985 and have personally witnessed the remarkable healing and transformation in her life. She refused to allow divorce and tragedy to defeat her, and as a result, she is now walking in her divine calling and destiny.

Debra is a Godly woman, a person of integrity, and a mighty preacher. I admire her passion for winning souls. When I think of Debra, I am reminded of Proverbs 11:30: "He who wins souls is wise". Thank you, Debra, for writing, **When Hurt Won't Stop**, and for being my faithful and trusted friend for over 30 years.

Lisa Osteen Comes
Associate Pastor, Lakewood Church

When Hurt Won't Stop reveals how God healed, filled, and restored the life of evangelist and soul winner, Debra George, after a traumatic divorce left her broken in heart and spirit. With brutal honesty, Debra recounts her transformational journey, as God's grace enabled her to travel through the agony of loss, adultery, confusion, and lack of self worth, into a position of victory, blessing and abundance through Christ. This is a must read if the loss of a marriage has left you trapped in a valley of despair! Debra's testimony will open your heart and mind to God's miracle working power amidst your greatest sorrow.

Pastor Paula White
Paula White Ministries

We have known, loved and believed in Debra for thirty years. She has demonstrated great courage to share her painful past, but she knows these keys will give you hope. After her book helps you survive, her preaching will help you thrive. Life is not fair, but God is good.

Pastors Tommy and Rachel Burchfield
Believer's World Outreach Church
Texas Bible Institute

When Hurt Won't Stop is a must-read for every person who desires to step out of the pain and disappointment of the past and into his/her God-given potential and future. In this book, Debra takes you through her own struggles of heartbreak, hurt and hopelessness to demonstrate how God can take past pain and turn it into present praise! She helps her readers realize that when it seems as though the hurt won't stop, God's getting ready to push you into greatness! When it looks like your life is over, Debra will show you how to WAKE UP YOUR DREAMS, how to live again, love again and run again with purpose. Debra is running fast for the Kingdom of God, raising up a soul winning army and she shows no signs of slowing down! I am sure this book will be a Word in due season for anyone who desires to walk in the fullness of his/her destiny!

Pastor Darlene Bishop
Solid Rock Church

Dedications

I would like to dedicate this book, first of all, to my parents. My beautiful mother, Donnie Modena Middlebrooks George, and my awesome father, Joe George, who always loved me, believed in me and sacrificed for me. I'll see you again in heaven.

I also dedicate this book to my entire family – which keeps on growing, because we love having babies. My love goes out to my awesome siblings: Andrew, Tena, Johnny Joe, and Jackie. Extended love to my sisters-in-law: Loveta, Annette and Eureta (Tijuana).

My deepest appreciation goes to Richard and Tena Ford. Thank you for picking me up off the ground when hard times hit.

Special thanks to my friends, who loved me and prayed with me during the tough times: Tommy & Rachel Burchfield, Lisa Osteen Comes, Linda Watson, Mark & Dena Trice, Spencer & Cyndy Nordyke, Debbi Urbano and so many others. I'll never forget what you did for me. I love you deeply!

A Note from Debra to You!

My purpose for writing this book is to give help and hope to you and your loved ones. If you have experienced the pain of divorce or a broken relationship, hang in there. Healing is available to you!

In no way is this book intended to elevate one person above another (Acts 10:34). God is NOT a respecter of persons. Nor is this book intended to give you a concrete plan of what to do when a mate walks out on you and your heart is broken. This is not a book of rules and regulations. It is not a book of bondage, restrictions or limitations. This is a book of freedom and healing.

Our lives are meant to be about following God and going all the way with Him, no matter what life may throw at us. I cannot tell you whether or not to stand for the restoration of a broken marriage. Nor do I mean to box anyone in, after a separation or divorce.

This book – simply put – is about how God led me to deal with and overcome four years of marital separation, which finally ended in divorce. A divorce I didn't want! A struggle in which I prayed everything I knew to pray. I stood on every scripture I could find. I attended every "Healing For Marriage" seminar that existed. Still things didn't go the way I wanted them to go. Why, God, why? How, God? How could this happen to me? God, what do I do now? How can I live with pain that will not stop? What do we do when life doesn't turn out the way we planned?

Let's take a journey that will surely move you from pain to purpose and from adversity to total victory. As for preparation, you can personalize your interaction with the book in one of two ways:

1. Journal your thoughts after each chapter as they relate to your own relationship experiences.

2. Use the *When Hurt Won't Stop Keys to Healing Relationship Pain Workbook*, which will supply prompts and key reviews to assist you.

Remember, it's not what happens to you in life that counts, but how you react to it!

TABLE OF CONTENTS

Introduction

1. I Never Thought It Could Happen To Me
2. Emotionally Out of Control
3. When Things Don't Go the Way You Planned
4. Please Pain! I'll Do Anything to Get Rid of You!
5. Trials are Transportation
6. The Craving for Intimacy
7. For Men Only!
8. Praying for Your Enemies
9. Heroes Stepping Up
10. A Prayer to be Healed!
11. You Have Value
12. It's Never Too Late!
13. Getting Your Stuff Back and More!
14. Be a Prisoner of Hope
15. Follow Your Passions
16. Wake Up Your Dream!

Introduction

The only thing I really wanted to succeed at was my marriage. And my marriage failed. I failed. I was down…past the point of depression. My thoughts were out of control. In fact, some days I wondered if my mind would suddenly snap and I would end up in an insane asylum.

Some advised me to see a psychiatrist. Though the medical profession has its place, God had a different idea. He led me on a journey that included His Word, prayer, intercession, holiness and a complete separation from the things of this world. I also underwent a parting of ways with every person who was not in agreement with the pathway I had chosen. It was Jesus and a handful of inner circle family members, pastors and friends who thrust me into my total restoration and healing.

I won't lie to you. It was a difficult journey in which I had few companions. It held many tears, fears and uncertainties about my future. But I made it! Today, I am happy, fulfilled, prosperous, blessed and preaching the Gospel of Jesus Christ all over the world. I am winning souls for Jesus, left and right. I live in a lovely home and am putting a substantial portion of my finances towards building a soul winning army across the world.

I don't see myself as a victim, as a survivor or as a second-class citizen. I further don't see myself as a failure or as someone who has the word, "divorce", stamped across my forehead. I tend to describe myself as a woman who has latched onto Jesus and His Word in her darkest hour. I am an overcomer through Jesus Christ!

I might also add, every hurt has been healed and the scrub brush of the Holy Spirit has erased every painful memory. I am free! I am anointed by God and on top of the world! Some religious mindsets may ask themselves, *"Can God use someone mightily who has gone through divorce?"* The answer can be stated simply, in one word…YES! Definitely, yes! Several women who proved the Lord right and the world wrong are in heaven today, complete with their rewards of fulfilling their life's calling. Kathryn Kuhlman and Aimee Semple McPherson are two, who come to mind. Oh! And let's not forget the woman at the well, in the Book of John, Chapter 4. This woman, who previously had five husbands, changed the world around her!

There are also many mighty men of God, with powerful ministries today, who were faced with the trials of broken relationships.

This is a book of hope. Hope for an incredible future with God, no matter what you've gone through. God is good…. all the time! Get ready for a new beginning! Let's start your life over again today – fresh and new. Your future is bright. The rest of your days are the best of your days. Hold your head up high. Everything changes – starting RIGHT NOW.

Chapter One

I Never Thought It Could Happen to Me

Once married, always married. That was the rule of thumb I was taught. My Dad (92 years of age) and my beautiful Mother, of 94 years, both recently went home to be with Jesus. He was a fiery Italian from Sicily, while she was friendly Irish. They were two opposites with a gigantic cultural challenge from the beginning. My Mother was the sixth of eleven children. She came from a family who was gentle, kind, loving, forgiving and soft-spoken. My Dad, the third of ten children, was loud, pushy, argumentative, and could hold a grudge against someone for years. But they both believed marriage was for a lifetime. In fact, divorce was never mentioned in our home.

My parents' beliefs are a large reason I always nestled the fairy tale, in my heart, of getting married, having children, and of course, LIVING HAPPILY EVER AFTER! When I found the man I believed was my life partner, I married at the age of 24. I couldn't have been happier! Both of us were believers, spirit-filled and called to minister to young people. To this day, I can't put my finger on what went wrong. Without any previous hint of discord, my husband walked through the door of our home one evening, announced that he didn't love me anymore and bluntly stated he wanted a divorce. I was beyond shock! How could this happen to me? This plot had no place in the fairy tale! I loved God, served Him every day and did everything I knew to be the perfect wife. The word "divorce" sent shivers coursing throughout my entire being.

As my world began to swirl out of control, I didn't know what to do. I tried reasoning with him. Nothing worked.

Later on, I found out my husband was involved with another woman. One sin in his life had led to another. He chose, at that point, to travel down a completely different pathway. Needless to say, this led to great pain and heartbreak for me. BUT WAIT JUST A MINUTE! The focus of this book is NOT defeat, but victory! I do not intend to put my husband down, or even to build myself up in your eyes. My intention, in telling my story, is to let you know I was faced with a myriad of decisions in the midst of my crisis.

Should I give up in an intense time of warfare?

Should I forget everything I knew about God's Word, just because I was being tested?

Should I break my marriage vows because I was hurting?

Could I stop serving God because I felt let down?

Could I stop loving my husband, just because he was breaking my heart?

Could I try retaliation and hurt him back?

Could I throw my Bible away and go back to the world?

Should I? Could I? Would I?

Something inside said, *"It's time to stand! It's time to fight back! It's time to get everything back that was stolen away!"*

After my husband's initial proclamation, I took several avenues of logic to try and negotiate with him, but I never got anywhere with my supplications. He said he never loved me to begin with. He went on to say, he didn't even want to sit on the same bed with me. He adamantly declared he was finished. Through an avalanche of words and tears, I mustered the strength to stumble to my car. Only then, did I realize it was two o'clock in the morning. I just started driving. But, where in the world do you go, when you really don't know whom you should turn to? My mind was so out of control, I couldn't think. Go to my parents? No! I just couldn't hurt them. And besides, I was too ashamed to tell them what had happened.

Suddenly, God's grace showed up. Somehow, the Holy Spirit guided the car and me to the home of Richard and Tena Ford. Not only are they precious family members, but wonderful pastors of a great church. The three of us prayed, cried and decided my marriage was worth standing for. More importantly, we agreed our God was worth serving, no matter what the future held!

Their wisdom, on that crazy day, still echoes in my mind today:

"Hold on, Debra. Hold on tight to Jesus! Read your Bible like there is no tomorrow. Pray, like a machine gun spraying bullets over a target, to override oppressive thoughts. Stay in church. We're here for you."

"Should I quit my teaching job?" I asked.

"No, no, no!" they said. "You need money to live on."

Life goes on and there are still bills to pay, no matter how heartbroken and desperate we may feel. As it turns out, keeping my job was the smartest thing I ever did!

I chose NOT to give up! My journey of standing and believing God for the restoration of my marriage was about to begin. I had no way of knowing how rough the next four years of my life would be. Looking back now, even though things were not resolved in the way I wanted then, I have never been sorry for one second of the experience. I made a life changing decision to stand on God's Word through trials and tests. It's always safe to trust Jesus, no matter how you respond emotionally.

Key #1

When your world swirls out of control, don't swirl with it!

Easier said than done, right? In practical terms, keep your job. Keep paying your bills. Stay in your church. Read your Bible, even when your eyes are too swollen from crying to see the scripture! Stay steady, steady, steady! God will see you through! He is faithful!

Chapter Two

Emotionally Out of Control!

I felt like a zombie! I rotated back and forth between experiencing almost unbearable pain, to not being able to feel anything at all. I totally related to Psalm 6:6 (KJV): "I am weary with my groaning: all the night I make my bed to swim; I water my couch with my tears". There were days when I graduated to a state of absolute numbness. I couldn't summon happiness, but I couldn't embrace sadness either. It was scary! Even so, I taught every day. I don't know how I kept my job. Honestly, you could say my Principal paid me for crying. I was a basket case – no good for anything or anyone – or so I thought!

I thank God for thinking differently than we do! No matter how badly we are hurting in life, God knows where we are. He reaches out to us! He specializes in turning trash into treasure. God sees great value in us. He has a specific future planned for all of his children, even though we may not be able to see it during the storm.

One of the hardest things I had to face, during my adjustment time, was living alone. Just when I thought I was fixed for life with the right partner – BAM! My life was suddenly and completely upside down! There were nights when I was so distraught I didn't think I was going to make it to sunrise. Many dark hours I cried, scraped my fingernails against the wall and held on – always hoping that somehow, some way, the pain would be taken from me. Thoughts of suicide tap-danced through my head, off and on for four years. All I can say, when I look back now, is thank You, Lord, for Your grace! Thank You for every single believer You prompted to intercede for me, during my bleakest nights and days! One reason I value men and women who intercede (pray seriously on behalf of others) is because I know the prayers of a saint are mighty. They push back the powers of darkness and chase away every plan of the enemy!

I believe the greatest action anyone can take, when emotionally out of control, as I was, is so basic that many miss it. It is simply to KEEP ON KEEPING ON! Don't do anything crazy or impulsive, such as quitting your job or immediately getting involved in another relationship. Sometimes, it's hard to admit to ourselves that we're not thinking straight. In order to avoid making bigger mistakes, it's best to stick, as close as we can, to our normal, established routine. I didn't stay in bed all day and cry, even if it was all I actually felt like doing. Instead, I got up every morning at the same time and tried to pray (though, some days, I cried more than I prayed). I felt like a total failure, but I still put one foot in front of the other and made my way to work each day.

My nights soon filled with God, God, God and more God. I read my Bible and stayed on my face before the Lord, crying out to Him continually. At some point during the night, He would lull me into a deep sleep. I guess He knew my body had to have rest, if I was going to win the battle. I tried to eat, but had zero appetite. I digested just enough to survive. This, of course, was not the right thing to do and I certainly don't recommend unhealthy behavior. Still, I know being truthful will speak to someone. I want you to know that everything did not fall into place immediately in the middle of my trial.

I read quite a few books during this lonely season of my life. Three of them stay prevalent:

Love Must Be Tough by Dr. James Dobson

Have You Felt Like Giving Up Lately? By David Wilkerson

Dream Seeds by Mike Murdock

I made it a practice to cram as much of the Word of God, as I could, into my spirit. Even on my breaks at school, I always had a purse full of mini-books that were jam-packed with scripture. I read to build my faith. I held onto Jesus with everything I had.

I experienced good days and terrible days. My thought life wandered through all kinds of attitudes, as I tried to get my feet back on solid ground. I eventually developed an opinion that Christian men were just as worldly as unsaved men. As a result of my wrong thinking, I chose to casually date two unsaved men after my divorce was final. Both of these guys thought I was beautiful. And yes! I have to admit I liked them, because I believed they would be instrumental in rebuilding my self-esteem. But the devil was slick and I found myself on the wrong road, being deceived by his lies. I had, somehow, embraced the idea that I couldn't make it without having a man in my life.

I celebrate the fact that God got tired of this very quickly. One day, shortly into my journey, He put His Foot down. I vividly remember driving down a road and hearing God speak (not audibly, but in my spirit). He said, *"Debra, do you want to lose everything again? Do you want your heart broken over and over?"*

"No, Lord, I don't!" I said out loud. He then spoke again. *"Let go of these relationships now or you will lose everything you have again."* That was all I needed to hear. I immediately shook myself back to reality and got back on the right track. I was hurting, but that did not give me the right to disobey God's Word. The Bible tells us, in 2 Corinthians 6:14, NOT to be unequally yoked together with an unbeliever. God's will is always His Word!

After I made the choice to come clean, so to speak, and remain IN the world, but not OF the world, I stepped over an unseen line. It was a faith-filled, commitment line that thrust me forward from defeat to victory. It moved me from hurt to healing. I also received a release from my previous torment to a peaceful life. BUT IT WASN'T OVER YET! God had some great things in store, just for me!

Key #2

Remember, you are not a failure!

You may see yourself as a failure. Remember, God does not intend you to live by your feelings, but by His Word! He lets us know, throughout the Bible, that He has a great future for you. Don't settle for anything less! Your enemy, the devil, has put up a smokescreen to try and cloud your vision. He wants you to believe the situation you are currently in is permanent. But Jesus tells us in John 8:44 that the devil is the father of all lies and a murderer from the beginning. Every day, thank God for a good life, the abundant life He has given you to richly enjoy! Just as I did, you will cross over a line into the joy, peace and blessings of Almighty God.

Chapter Three

When Things Don't Go the Way You Planned

What a great place to be! Really. I'm not kidding with you! I'm looking back on a four-to-five year painful, heart-wrenching season of my life and I'm so happy today. Nothing in this previous season of life turned out the way I planned, so I simply got busy living. But, I'm referring to living purposely. Jesus says, in John 10:10 (NKJV), "The thief does not come except to steal, and to kill, and to destroy. I have come that they may have life, and that they may have it more abundantly."

I love how the Amplified Bible translates the latter part of this verse: " I came that they may have and enjoy life, and have it in abundance [to the full, till it overflows]." Clearly, God's will for all is to have life until it overflows, but that can only happen when we operate in God's plan for our lives. My plan didn't work out. Possibly your plans aren't working out either. But that makes us perfect candidates to start functioning inside God's. "As for God, His way is perfect!" (Psalms 18:30a)

Soon, I found myself stepping into God's instructions for my life. To my shock and surprise, He called me out of a full time teaching job to travel across the world, winning souls and preaching the Gospel of Jesus Christ. Today, I continue to tell everyone I meet about the goodness of God and His wonderful plan of restoration for our lives. God can, and will, do exceedingly, abundantly, above all we can ask, hope for, dream about or think. (Ephesians 3:20)

Everything I inherited, as a result of my divorce, is no longer a part of my life – poverty, lack, debt, a small apartment and a car (that broke down constantly). God has blessed me with a beautiful home on a lake, where I sit and watch the ducks swim by, as I laugh in the devil's face and remind him of God's Word. No weapon, devil, formed against me will prosper. It didn't work, devil! And you will pay every day for trying to destroy me! I am blessed, financially, and in every other way. God has stepped in. His plan prevailed in my life. Go ahead. Take a deep breath and tell God, "Okay, Lord, I surrender my plan and my will to you. I can't make things work out right. I need your help, Jesus. Will you please help me, Lord?" Get ready. God will take control of your life, as well as everything and every one who concerns you. He will rearrange your life to become something beautiful.

Key #3

**When things don't turn out the way you've planned,
it is time to look toward Heaven and smile real big!**

You might ask, how can I smile? Or better yet, why would I smile? Just smile. Your plans didn't work out, but rest assured, this means God has a better plan for your life. Exchange your plan for His plan. He has a wonderful idea, up His sleeve, which will bring you so much joy. You'll look back someday and be glad your plans failed.

Chapter Four

Please Pain! I'll Do Anything to Get Rid of You!

It's still hard for me to believe THE PAIN IS GONE! I'm not kidding! I hurt so badly, for so many years, I honestly didn't know if I would ever be happy again! Thank God for His grace. Grace, grace and more grace was, and still is, all over my life. It's all over your life, too! God's grace is precious, mostly because we can't earn it and we don't deserve it. Grace, defined, is when God chooses to be good to us, even though, sometimes, He should really knock us upside our heads (that's Clodine, Texas talk). Because God is good, He gives us special favor. He stands prepared to walk with us through difficult times to victory. Just when I couldn't go another step, God would pick me up and carry me, just like the familiar poem, *Footprints in the Sand*.

I'm so pain free and full of joy, as I write this today, I have to stop and crack up laughing. It's so hard for me to believe that I ever hurt so deeply. It's almost as if the entire experience never happened to me. That's how completely healed I am today. Glory be to the only One who can keep us from falling, the Lord Jesus Christ!

The point I want to stress, most of all, is the fact that I didn't become pain free or full of joy overnight. Oh, how I wish there was some special formula I could share with you, to make your pain go away instantly. If there were such, I would have given everything I owned, at the time, for the remedy. I would have taken a car, plane, boat or train to the other side of the world to buy it! But the truth of the matter is simply this: Jesus and time are the best painkillers. You must have Jesus to be healed and you must have time to be completely restored.

There are four things I did that brought me from pain and desperation to total healing, joy and victory.

I stayed extremely close to my local church.

Your church is a place of safety. This is where your spiritual family resides. This is where you can hear God's Word, be prayed for, be cared for and where you can receive the supporting love you need. Every time the doors opened for services, I was there. No matter how weak I was or how bad I looked, I simply went to church. Because of my persistence and consistence in church attendance, God was able to bring me to complete healing. Just go to church. This will give God an opportunity to straighten out your mess.

I spent time alone with God.

I read my Bible. I prayed like there was no tomorrow. I was literally fighting for my life. The scripture, John 14:14, tells us we can ask Jesus for anything and He will do it for us. I focused on God, God and more of God. The more I dove into the Word and into prayer, the more I began to see how much bigger God was than my problems. This led me to victory.

I surrounded myself with believers who would be encouragers.

Proverbs 13:20 (NKJV) states: "He who walks with wise men will be wise, but the companion of fools shall be destroyed." In other words, choosing your company wisely will help you to grow stronger in God than ever before. I avoided (at all costs) ANYONE who spoke defeat to me. I surrounded myself with strong men and women of God. If you do this, you are on your way to victory!

I kept reminding myself that pain was temporary.

Joy is coming! Psalm 23:4 (AKJV) is a great reminder! "Yes, though I walk through the valley of the shadow of death, I will fear no evil: for you are with me; your rod and your staff, they comfort me." Remember, Jesus never leaves us in the valley. He is taking us *through* the valley to the other side, where our lives will, once again, be filled with joy! Hold on! Pain is temporary! God's joy is permanent! Don't give up! Stand on the Word and fight the good fight of faith. (1 Timothy 6:12)

Though it may seem to you that hurt and pain won't stop, I want to remind you that what you are facing is only for a season. I encourage you to take this opportunity to dig your heels in and grow spiritually like never before. Wear your Bible out! Take notes at church. Listen to God's Word on your way to work. Grow! Grow! Grow! Everything you do in this time period is coming together to form an amazing future for you!

Key #4

The Word of God is your best medicine!

Dive into God's Word – every morning, every night – and as often as you can in between. Fill up on His Word! Speak those scripture passages that apply to your situation out loud. Remember the power of God's Word. Here is a great example to nestle into your heart, mind and soul. "For the Word of God is living and powerful, and sharper than any two-edged sword, piercing even to the division of soul and spirit, and of joints and marrow, and is a discerner of the thoughts and intents of the heart." The Word will bring you into victory every time!

Chapter Five

Trials are Transportation

God's purpose for our lives is to help others. The entire time I was praying for God to restore my marriage, He had a secret desire for my life. The Bible says, in Isaiah 55:8-9 (RSV), "For my thoughts are not your thoughts, neither are your ways my ways, says the Lord. For as heavens are higher than the earth, so are my ways higher than your ways, and my thoughts than your thoughts." I am guilty of trying to get my plan to work for my life. I thought my husband would come back home. I thought our marriage would be restored and we would live happily ever after. Boy, was I ever wrong! You might be tempted to ask, "Debra, why didn't your husband come home? After all, isn't that what you prayed for?" The only answer I have for you is simple. I DON'T KNOW! But, what I DO know is this: Our God is a good God! He had a bigger, better, more awesome plan for my life than I could have ever dreamed possible. Just when I thought my life was over, God let me know that we were just beginning! Jesus sees much farther down the road than we can. He knows what is up ahead and what is best for us! It is why Jesus is often called, The Alpha and the Omega. These are Greek terms, meaning the first and the last. Jesus is the Beginning and the End! He knows everything! I may not understand everything – but I don't have to. When we don't understand, we only have to trust God! Trust in your loving, Heavenly Father, who has only your best interests in mind. Proverbs 3:5-6 (NJKV) gives us this instruction: "Trust in the Lord with all your heart, and lean not on your own understanding. In all your ways acknowledge him, and he shall direct your paths." No matter what happens, trust Him!

My divorce finalized. *Oh no! This is not what I wanted!* My body was weakened by the news. My mind was frazzled. I held onto the walls, again, just to make it through my nights. I wanted to die. I was so afraid of my future. I felt insecure and unsure about life.

Eventually, I recognized that fear is a great source of torment, but it is not from God. In fact, God has not given any of us a spirit of fear. I studied II Timothy 1:7 (NKJV), which says, " For God has not given us a spirit of fear, but of power, and of love and of a sound mind." I decided to stand on the Word. I decided to hold onto Jesus with everything in me. I purposed to get my fight back!

In the beginning, every night, I went to sleep crying. Every morning, I woke up crying. After the divorce, I asked the Lord, *"What happened? I did my very best to see to it that my marriage worked out. I prayed. I fasted. I kept my life pure. I stood on Your Word, Lord. I did my best! What happened?"* I hardly spoke all the words before the Lord responded to me. *"Debra, I did my best, too!"* Wow! Jesus gave our marriage His best shot, too! That was all I needed to hear. As I realized Jesus loved me enough to do His best for me, I immediately felt better. I knew He was not holding anything back.

And Jesus never withholds anything from those who walk upright before Him. He not only loves you enough to do His best for you – He loves you too much! He loves us more than we can ever imagine. Whatever we are trusting Him to do, today, we can know He is moving on our behalf. He is in the background of our lives, arranging the best possible plan for us. It's not easy to trust – especially when we are feeling vulnerable. But, as much as is possible within you, give yourself and your entire life to Jesus

Christ. I guarantee, in the end, your situation will turn out for the glory of God and the furtherance of His Kingdom.

Not long after this encounter with God, His ideas for my life started unfolding. God instructed me to resign my teaching job. I began to travel across the states, and around the world, winning souls and preaching the Gospel of Jesus Christ.

When I look back to the day I opened my mailbox and saw those divorce papers, I can throw back my head and laugh. When I remember the painful, sleepless nights, filled with thoughts of suicide, I drop down to my knees and thank my God that His plans (and not mine) have come to pass. Only God – and He alone – knows what is best for our lives. I can see, now, God used my trial for transportation to get me to the place, within His Kingdom, which was exactly where He wanted me to be. What an awesome God we serve!

Psalm Twenty-Three becomes more and more meaningful to me each day. Though you walk through the valley of the shadow of death, don't fear. Today, God will not leave you in the valley. You are going through to the other side, where the grass is green and life is abundant and overflowing. Many make the mistake of stopping in the valley. We all know people who are "valley stayers", instead of "valley passer throughers". How sad it is to see someone throw away the rest of their lives, just because they have to travel through a few valleys and face a few storms. Unfortunately, some stay so long in the valley they build hotels. You can recognize those who have stopped at the point of a divorce, stopped at bankruptcy, stopped at rejection or stopped when life turned an unexpected corner. Today, I'm encouraging YOU. Don't stop! Don't ever quit! Your breakthrough is right around the next bend. The rest of your days are the best of your days! You'll never know what God has for you, until you push forward to receive His very best. I love how the psalmist talks about how goodness and mercy will follow us all the days of our lives. When we are in the valley, we may feel alone, yet, as we walk out, we can hear double footsteps. There is something echoing behind us. Who can be following now? Glancing back, over the difficult experiences of my life, I can see goodness and mercy have traveled through every single valley with me. After all, you never see anything growing on top of a mountain. It is only in the valleys where we grow and learn to trust God as never before.

The mountaintops are there so we can stand and look down at the valleys and remember how the goodness of our God brought us through!

Key #5

When it looks like your life is over, don't believe it!

This is a lie from the devil! God is not holding any good thing back from you. He is preparing a great future for you. He has a perfect plan for your life! Thank Him, right now, for bringing you into His "God Ideas" and for the plan He has for you.

Chapter Six

The Craving for Intimacy

Every person craves intimacy. It's the way God made us. Years of having an intimate relationship with my husband (and suddenly having that taken away) presented some challenges in my life. Many may ask, "How on earth can anyone who once experienced the joy and pleasure of a sexual relationship find fulfillment without this type of intimacy?"

Jesus explains it best, in II Corinthians 12:9, when He says, "My grace is sufficient for you." Who can understand the grace of God? The answer is so easy that sometimes, I think, all believers overlook it. NO human being, no matter how close to God we may think we are, can ever grasp His limitless grace. Grace is something so precious (and so divinely given by God) that it cannot be understood nor figured out by human minds – no matter how intelligent we might be or how many degrees or PhD's we may have accumulated. The grace of God can never be figured out. It must be experienced.

I have never been able to understand God's grace. I can't imagine why He could love us so much! I don't think I will ever have the answers. But what I DO know is this: I am the recipient of the grace of God and BECAUSE OF HIS GRACE, I was able to go on with life and not feel or notice any lack.

I'm sure you've heard the word "grace" defined. And, even with as many definitions as we've all heard, I can sum them all up, by saying God's grace is "the filler" that completes every area of our lives, including those we could never fill or make complete on our own. Grace is not a state of working or doing; grace is a state of being.

In other words, I could not rid myself of a desire for sexual intimacy with a man. People have these desires, because they are God-given. God created these desires, but – and here is the key – the same God Who created the desire and appetite for intimacy is also the God Who can – and will – fill any emptiness or void in this area of our lives when a marriage dissolves – whether through divorce or the death of a mate.

God's grace is a FILLER, shoring up every empty place in our lives. He doesn't leave anything incomplete. He FILLS our lives. The Word of God tells us, in Colossians 2:10 (NKJV), "and you are complete in Him, who is the head of all principality and power."

This particular definition of grace is not something I learned from any book or in any classroom. I've experienced this kind of grace and you can experience it too! How? WHEN –AND ONLY WHEN – YOU STOP TRYING TO FIX YOURSELF AND EVERYONE AROUND YOU. Go ahead and admit this to God right now, just like I had to do. "Lord, I can't fix myself. I'm just in too big a mess. I'm too needy. I'm too brokenhearted. I'm too rejected. I'm too down on myself. My self-esteem is so low; I have no esteem left at all. I have too many empty places in my life that I can't fix or fill. Lord, I need You. I need Your help. I need Your fillers. I need Your GRACE! I can't fix my husband. I can't make him change. I can't make him come home. I can't make him want me. I can't take away his desire and lust for other women. I can't fix this, Lord. I can't make everything all right again. Lord, please help me. I have no control over this. I'm hoping that it's just a bad dream and that I'll wake up soon. But, as every day passes, Lord, I realize this is no dream. This is really happening and as each day goes by, I also realize the only way I'm going to get through it all is to admit I can't fix this one. I've got to go to the ROCK that is HIGHER than I am. I've got to step ONTO THE ROCK THAT IS CHRIST JESUS. All else is sinking sand. Oh God, I must have your grace to fill every area of my life. Thank you so much for Your grace!"

In the meantime, while I was the recipient of His grace, I made some changes in my life. I reevaluated myself. I shut myself off from as much of this world as was humanly possible.

The Word of God says we are IN the world, not OF the world. That can be confusing. *Whatever do you mean, Debra, about shutting yourself off from the world? We have to live in the world!* Let me explain. On my way to work each day, I cried out to God in my car. While I ironed my clothes in the morning, I cried out to God. On my break at school, I chose to stuff myself with the Word of God, instead of food. When I returned home in the evening, the television stayed off. I ignored all of the emotional phone calls from family and friends, as well as the worldly advice from well-meaning Christians. I only picked up the phone when I heard the familiar voice of an encouraging family member or friend who loved me and was genuinely praying for me.

Instead of the television, I chose to put a small towel on my bedroom floor. I fell on my face before God, allowing my tears to flow. I cried freely, not holding any emotion back. My workday was over and there were no people around to create concern with what someone might think of me or have to listen to what they thought I ought to be doing. The evenings consisted of me, my God, my Bible and a small towel to soak up the tears. I stayed on the floor until I knew the devil's thoughts had left and that God's peace had filled my troubled mind. I kept my face buried in the towel until I knew I would make it through the night.

Torment is a terrible, evil thing from a terrible, evil enemy: the devil. I experienced torment. I wondered if I would make it through the night. The Bible says, in Psalm 30:5, that weeping may endure for the night, but joy comes in the morning. But, like Pastor Richard Ford, a great man of God, taught me: "How long is the night, Lord?" My "night" lasted for about four years. I battled thoughts of suicide and temptations of all kinds. I thought of everything from marrying an unsaved man to just disappearing inside a foreign country and changing my name along the way. I thought about going to a bar and getting totally drunk, until I fell off a bar stool and didn't know, any longer, who I was. I thought about letting my mind go totally crazy, until I was strapped in a straight jacket in some insane asylum, not knowing, or even caring, what my name was. I thought about undergoing shock treatment in the hope that all of the painful memories would leave.

I couldn't help but remember a friend who had shock treatment in order to forget her husband's affair. She forgot how to drive her car and even how to get to the corner store by her home. She forgot a lot of things, but the one thing she remembered was her husband's affair. The world's type of shock treatment will mess you up, but God's healing treatment will fix you up.

Thank God I didn't do any of the things I thought about doing. I could have and would have broken my fellowship with God and nothing is worth that. If you fall and make a mistake, get up again. God is merciful. He forgives. He restores. He makes brand new!

Today, I am healed! Many of the painful memories are truly forgotten! In fact, some people probably think I've had shock treatment, but I haven't. I've been to hell and back. What I've learned didn't come out of a textbook. It came from experiencing real pain. All I've had, all along, is Jesus, my Bible and my towel.

    I made changes. Even to this day, I am cautious about what I allow my eye to see and my ears to hear. I won't watch any type of program that makes light of marriage; people sleeping around with someone they are not married to. Call me old-fashioned if you want, but I don't find these types of things entertaining. It really happened to me and I wasn't part of a movie. I don't watch anything that is sinful, has bad language or that is not pure. My life, destiny, future, calling, anointing and thoughts are more valuable to me, than a few minutes of entertainment. For me, these things are sin. For you, they may not be sin and that's fine. No problem. Enjoy your movies. I'm not trying to make you like me. I don't want you to fit into my mold or what I think you should be or do. That's not my motive for sharing these intimate things with you about my life. What I am trying to do is to tell you how God led me into a total healing, victory and restoration for my life. The way God leads you may, or may not, be the way He led me. And that's perfectly okay.

God made each of us individuals. He has a master plan for your life – and yours alone. But, here's where the importance of the towel comes to bear. It was during the times I fell on my face daily that I received God's instructions and His battle plan for what I was facing. I received strict, detailed instructions from Heaven that I followed until every "t" was crossed and every "i" was dotted. I am a winner today, not because I tried to do what someone else did, in his or her own situation, but because I did what God told me to do in my own situation. That is what has made the difference in my life.

Remember, it is not enough to hear God's battle plan. Once you hear, you must obey. Isaiah 1:19 states: if you are WILLING AND OBEDIENT you will eat the good of the land. It's not enough to be willing. Willing is a good start, but after willingness, obedience must follow in order to get God's VERY, VERY BEST for our lives. Unfortunately, many Christians have lived and died and will continue to live and die with a wonderful willingness, but have never prioritized or put God's instructions, over and above man's opinions. Therefore, they have lived their entire lives without entering into God's best. They lived their whole lives without ever entering into His perfect will for their lives.

Fear of man, or what others might think or say, stops many people from being obedient to instructions that come from God. May I give a word of advice to you? Throw caution to the wind. Risk being laughed at, made fun of, or talked about. Risk the chance of being misunderstood. Even risk the chance of losing favor with a family member, close friend, church member, employee or co-worker. BUT NEVER, EVER risk the chance of losing your favor with God, your Creator, and THE LOVER OF YOUR SOUL. Do whatever He tells you to do and you will, without a doubt, enter into God's best. God told me to stand for my marriage. I did that for four years. There were others around me who thought I shouldn't have stood that long and believed for my husband to return. You can see, that no matter what you do, you will never make everyone happy. Your focus must be making God happy. And when you make Him happy, nothing else matters.

Don't ever make the mistake of fearing man. The fear of man creates a snare. It traps you and brings you into bondage. You can spend your whole life trying to make others happy or pleased with you and your decisions, only to find they still don't understand you. Forget it! You're trying too hard! Relax. Let God fix everything and everyone, including you. Like my dear friend, Jesse Duplantis, says, "Your only job is to let God do His job." Be blessed today. Pray right now and ask God to deliver you from the fear and opinions of man. Come on, shake free! Move toward the place where God wants you to be. Move toward the position, the state of being, where God, your Father, your Creator is happy and pleased with you.

I have found, when God is happy with me, He causes everyone around me to be happy with me, too! When a man's ways please the Lord He can, and will, make even his enemies to be at peace with him. When you have someone around you that can't handle the fact that God is happy with you, many times, He will move them right out of your life. There's not a thing in the world wrong with that! After all, what good does it do for any of us to look alive on the outside, but yet be dead on the inside? Even if I succeed in pulling that charade off and making others think I'm happy and okay, God knows the real truth. He knows how we're doing all the time. To be honest with you, He's the only One who really counts. Focus on God's will being done in your life.

God's ways are not our ways. Why would God have me stand in a marriage for four years, when it never came back together? Could it possibly be God wanted me to focus on Him for four years? Is it possible that God knew fighting for my marriage would cause me to draw nearer to Him than I ever had been in all of my life? After all is said and done, He is God and He knows what we need and when we need it. We must learn to trust Him in a greater way!

Come on! Stir yourself up!!! Shout out loud! I WANT GOD'S BEST FOR MY LIFE, no matter who it separates me from or joins me to. TAKE THAT DEVIL! In Jesus' Name! So be it in my life!

Key #6

You Are NOT Alone!

God is with you and you must fall on God's grace. Admit right now that you cannot make it by yourself. You can't get where you need to go on your own. Ask God for His grace to help you. His grace is sufficient for you. His grace is made perfect in your weakness.

Chapter Seven

For Men Only!

There's nothing cute, funny or macho about adultery. The ways of the world are not the ways of God. Every man should live a clean, pure life that is pleasing to God. Married men are to remain faithful and true to their respective wives. Every unmarried man is to serve God without distraction. These lifestyle habits are outlined clearly, in accordance with His Word. If every man would read his Bible every day and live his life by what he learned, there would be no extra-marital affairs. There would be fewer divorces and fewer wives with broken hearts and distrust for husbands, and men in general.

Nothing but the grace of God qualifies me to dedicate an entire chapter to men. I watched the man I loved fall into the devil's trap of the adulterous woman. She is clearly described in the Book of Proverbs.

Proverbs 5 (AMPC)

1 MY SON, be attentive to my Wisdom [godly Wisdom learned by actual and costly experience], and incline your ear to my understanding [of what is becoming and prudent for you],

2 That you may exercise proper discrimination and discretion and your lips may guard and keep knowledge and the wise answer [to temptation].
3 For the lips of a loose woman drip honey as a honeycomb, and her mouth is smoother than oil;
4 But in the end she is bitter as wormwood, sharp as a two-edged and devouring sword.
5 Her feet go down to death; her steps take hold of Sheol (Hades, the place of the dead).
6 She loses sight of and walks not in the path of life; her ways wind about aimlessly, and you cannot know them.
7 Now therefore, my sons, listen to me, and depart not from the words of my mouth.
8 Let your way in life be far from her, and come not near the door of her house [avoid the very scenes of temptation],
9 Lest you give your honor to others and your years to those without mercy,
10 Lest strangers [and false teachings] take their fill of your strength and wealth and your labors go to the house of an alien [from God] –
11 And you groan and mourn when your end comes, when your flesh and body are consumed,
12 And you say, How I hated instruction and discipline, and my heart despised reproof!
13 I have not obeyed the voice of my teachers nor submitted and consented to those who instructed me.
14 [The extent and boldness of] my sin involved almost all evil [in the estimation] of the congregation and the community.
15 Drink waters out of your own cistern [of a pure marriage relationship], and fresh waters out of your own well.
16 Should your offspring be dispersed abroad as water brooks in the streets?
17 [Confine yourself to your own wife] let your children be for you alone, and not the children of strangers with you.
18 Let your fountain [of human life] be blessed [with the rewards of fidelity], and rejoice in the wife of your youth.
19 Let her be as the loving hind and pleasant doe [tender, gentle, attractive] – let her bosom satisfy you at all times, and always be transported with delight in her love.

20 Why should you, my son, be infatuated with a loose woman, embrace the bosom of an outsider, and go astray?
21 For the ways of man are directly before the eyes of the Lord, and He [Who would have us live soberly, chastely, and godly] carefully weighs all man's goings.
22 His own iniquities shall ensnare the wicked man, and he shall be held with the cords of his sin.
23 He will die for lack of discipline and instruction, and in the greatness of his folly he will go astray and be lost.

Proverbs 6:32-35 (AMPC)

32 But whoever commits adultery with a woman lacks heart and understanding (moral principle and prudence); he who does it is destroying his own life.
33 Wounds and disgrace will he get, and his reproach will not be wiped away.
34 For jealousy makes [the wronged] man furious; therefore he will not spare the day of vengeance [upon the detected one].
35 He will not consider any ransom [offered to buy him off from demanding full punishment]; neither will he be satisfied, though you offer him many gifts and bribes.

The Word of God is powerful and, not only that, it is our instruction book for life. After seeing the man I loved sucked into a vacuum created by a beautiful woman, I understood the meaning of the Proverbs scripture, where it says the adulteress would hunt for the precious life. Men – your life, your marriage, your children, your calling and – more importantly – your relationship with God is PRECIOUS!

I would like to tell you that the adulterous woman is an idiot and ugly. And even tell you she is stupid or unintelligent. But this is simply never the truth! The adulterous woman is usually beautiful, seductive and extremely smart. She is on a major hunt. Her method is not much different than a man who loves to hunt deer, elk, birds or coon. (As you may be able to tell, I'm from Texas.) Just as the hunting of wild game is a sport many consider an enjoyable pastime, adultery is the adulterous woman's sport. Don't kid yourselves, men. She is ready and willing to go to any length to pick out her target, adjust her scope and aim her bullet until she gets exactly who and what she wants.

I learned the hard way how to recognize this woman from a distance. I see her on the streets, in places of business, in the shopping malls, the gym, and yes …even in our churches. She is everywhere. She is perpetually hunting and her goal is to take down a man – YOUR precious life! Every woman who is reading this (because I know you couldn't resist)…stop right now and ask God to enable you to identify her. Recognizing her early on could save your husband and your marriage.

On the outside, she can appear so harmless. Gentlemen, she can pretend to be your wife's best friend. She can sing in the choir. Yet, on the inside, she is full of lust and just waiting for the right opportunity to make herself available to you. Watch her! Run from her! Stay away from her! And never, ever allow yourself to be alone with her. You may not be able to stop her from working at your company or from attending your church. You may not be able to force her to move out of your neighborhood. But there is one thing you can do! You can live as Proverbs 4:25 (NKJV) instructs: "Let your eyes look straight ahead, and your eyelids look right before you." Run in the opposite direction every time you sense she may be near you.

Also, please gentlemen, never allow any woman to share with you the problems she is having concerning her marriage, that is, without the presence of your wife by your side. Should a woman approach you, wanting you to listen to her, pray for her or give her counsel when your wife is not present, don't allow it! Graciously interrupt her and send her straight to another woman for help.

Don't open yourself up. Don't do it! I know what you might be thinking. *I'm a strong man. I can take it. I'll never cheat on my wife.* Please understand that many men have fallen into the trap of sexual sin while having these same, prideful, thoughts. Guard yourself and protect your thought life. Don't allow your mind to go in the direction of entertaining another woman. Pastors and leaders, stop meeting with women alone! Stop it right now! She is a trap and you should never meet with any woman - I REPEAT - any woman, without being in the presence of your wife. If you are single, Pastor, then bring in your sister, mother or somebody female, but don't open the door for the enemy.

The relationship you have with your wife is a covenant.

Ephesians 5:25-33 (AMPC) is worth reviewing here:

25 Husbands, love your wives, as Christ loved the church and gave Himself up for her,
26 So that He might sanctify her, having cleansed her by the washing of water with the Word,
27 That He might present the church to Himself in glorious splendor, without spot or wrinkle or any such things [that she might be holy and faultless].
28 Even so husbands should love their wives as [being in a sense] their own bodies. He who loves his own wife loves himself.
29 For no man ever hated his own flesh, but nourishes and carefully protects and cherishes it, as Christ does the church.
30 Because we are members (parts) of His body.

31 For this reason a man shall leave his father and his mother and shall be joined to his wife, and the two shall become one flesh.
32 This mystery is very great, but I speak concerning [the relationship of] Christ and the church.
33 However, let each man of you [without exception] love his wife as [being in a sense] his very own self; and let the wife see that she respects and reverences her husband [that she notices him, regards him, honors him, prefers him, venerates and esteems him; and that she defers to him, praises him, and loves and admires him exceedingly].

The goal of the adulterous woman is to break up and to destroy something so pure, so sacred, and so very God-given. I'll never forget, after my husband left me, he still had a key to the apartment that we once shared. One day, when I returned home from teaching school, I walked through my door and immediately knew she had been there. I guess my husband brought her with him to leave some of his belongings, as we had pre-arranged. He was in the process of relocating and wanted to store some things with me. As I went from room to room, I noticed all of the photos, those only of my husband and I, were turned around backwards. My spare closet held his briefcase. When I opened it, I saw it was filled with love letters written to him by her. When I dug though another box placed beside the case, I found pornographic magazines –

placed either knowingly or unknowingly by either or both of them. I cried and shook until I wasn't sure whether life was worth living or not. The letters and magazines seemed to knock the wind out of me. Even in this moment of my weakness, I began to get angry inside. I was angry at sin, angry at what the enemy was doing to my husband and trying to do to me. Somehow or another, I mustered up enough strength to place the briefcase, letters and magazines into garbage bags and throw them into the front yard for my garbage service to pick up the next day. I didn't want anything so wicked to stay in my apartment overnight.

I share these things with you, gentlemen, so that perhaps you'll look further down the road to just where an adulterous woman wants to take you. Train yourselves, early on, so that you can see where her compliments and her good looks will lead. She is the road to destruction.

Proverbs 6:26 (AMPC) says: "For on account of a harlot a man is brought to a piece of bread, and the adulteress stalks and snares [as with a hook] the precious life [of a man]." Study this scripture until you can quote it in your sleep. This Word will save your life and your marriage. Ask God to help you recognize a woman who has evil intentions towards you and your marriage. The God who helped Joseph to flee from Potiphar's wife is the same God who will help you to run also, before it's too late.

Think of Joseph for a moment. I'm sure Potiphar's wife was beautiful to look upon. Think of how easily Joseph could have yielded to this temptation and sin. Think of how any man can have an affair, but it takes a strong man of God – with a lot of character and backbone – to flee and to say no to temptation and evil. Read Genesis, Chapter 39, for the complete story of how Joseph fled from temptation.

I, personally, don't have anything against the adulterous woman. She is greatly loved by Jesus. She needs His help and His mercy. Breaking up someone else's marriage can never fulfill her life. Another person is never our enemy. The Bible tells us in Ephesians 6:12 that we are not fighting against flesh and blood. Our only enemy is the devil, who is the driving force behind every adulterous woman. Jesus loves this woman and I learned to love her, too.

There is forgiveness, hope, and healing, along with total restoration for any woman or man who has ever fallen into the trap of adultery. God forgave and restored David in the Bible. He can and will forgive and restore you, too! Just ask Jesus to help you and He will. Ask Jesus to deliver you and He will. Identify someone in your church who is trustworthy and who will stand with you and pray with you. You need the help of another strong believer in Jesus. Ask God to show you who you can trust. When you know whom that person is, lean on them in times of weakness. One day you will be strong in this area and someone will be able to lean on you. In II Corinthians 1: 4 (NKJV), Paul tells us Jesus will be the One: "who comforts us in all our tribulation, that we may be able to comfort those who are in any trouble, with the comfort with which we ourselves are comforted by God."

Key #7

Base your whole life on God's Word, not on your opinions, feelings or emotions.

When we read Psalm 119:105 (NKJV), we learn, "Your word is a lamp to my feet, and a light to my path." Let God's Word shine His light on you and every relationship you have with family and friends. God's Word is your standard in which to live by.

Chapter Eight

Praying for Your Enemies

During the years I stood for the restoration of my marriage, God taught me how to pray for the other woman. This was a most painful process, yet most fruitful. Today, I love everybody – no matter who anyone might be or what he/she may have done. I can honestly say I love you, too! No strings attached. I love every person with an unconditional love and I am free to express this love to every person who crosses my path. I love people in general! You don't have to be like me for me to love you. I love!

Allow me to share the secret to loving everyone, even your enemies. I received this ability to love during those long, lonely nights I spent praying on my face, before God. I was infused with this love straight from Jesus, while I prayed for the other woman. Jesus instructs us well in Luke 6:27-28 (AMPC): "But I say to you who are listening now to Me: [in order to heed, make it a practice to] love your enemies, treat well (do good to, act nobly toward) those who detest you and pursue you with hatred. Invoke blessings upon and pray for the happiness of those who curse you, implore

God's blessing (favor) upon those who abuse you [who revile, reproach, disparage, and high-handedly misuse you]."

God has given me such love! If I were to bump into her today, I could greet her with a pure heart, filled with the love of God. My desire for her is that she has prosperity, blessings, happiness and fulfillment. I hold absolutely nothing against her. After all, we all make mistakes. We've all sinned in one area or another. Romans 3:23 (NIV) says: "for all have sinned and fall short of the glory of God."

I should sum it up by saying this. I refuse to be a bitter, hurt and unforgiving person. I refuse to live with a victim mentality. Instead, I prefer to have a victor's mentality. It's all because of the grace of God. His grace fills in all of the empty, hurtful areas of our lives. I'm so free from all of the hurt, that if I ever did see the other woman again, I'd actually like to thank her! Thank her for exposing something in my husband's life that I didn't know was there. My life has turned out so much greater than I could ever have imagined. The affair she had with my husband forced me on my face, before God, to seek Him like I had never sought Him before. Because of all of the things that went wrong, God was able to steer me in the right direction – down on my knees. Your friends will take you to coffee. Your enemies will force you on your face before God. That's why, many times, your enemies are more beneficial to your spiritual growth.

II Corinthians 2:14 (AMPC) says: "But thanks be to God, Who in Christ always leads us in triumph [as trophies of Christ's victory] and through us spreads and makes evident the fragrance of the knowledge of God everywhere."

Key #8

Pray for those who hurt you.

Pray for them everyday and watch God turn things around inside you. Something supernatural happens when we pray for those who have talked badly about us or wronged us in some way. Jesus instructs us, in the Word of God, to pray for our enemies and for those who despitefully use us. When we are obedient to do what He wants us to do, He will bring great favor into our lives.

Chapter Nine

Heroes Stepping Up

One morning my phone rang. The familiar voice of my dear friend, Rachel Burchfield, was a welcome start to my day. "Debra," she said, "I have a scripture for you today. It's Hebrews 10:35-36."

I grabbed my Bible and read from the Amplified Classic (AMPC) Bible translation: "Do not, therefore, fling away your fearless confidence, for it carries a great and glorious compensation of reward. For you have need of steadfast patience and endurance, so that you may perform fully and accomplish the will of God, and thus receive and carry away [and enjoy to the full] what is promised."

As Rachel told me, time and time again, "Don't give up, Debra." I would always respond to her, "I won't, Rachel." That very day, as I was on the phone and unbeknownst to me, God was about to use Rachel to divinely connect me to a woman of God who would deposit an anointing into my life and become one of my nearest and dearest lifetime friends. Her name was Lisa Osteen, now Lisa Comes. Rachel shared, as we talked, about how God was using Lisa at Lakewood Church on Tuesday nights in a ministry called, The Healing Center for Marriages. Rachel said, "Debra, you need to go. Can I tell Lisa that you'll come this week?" I agreed to attend.

To be honest with you, I had been invited to The Healing Center by other friends, previously. I had no desire to go. I thought it might be a meeting similar to Alcoholics Anonymous where I would have to get up in front of people and tell everyone how my husband left me and that he was currently seeing another woman. The very thought of having to do this sent a cold chill down my spine. I was already ashamed and embarrassed enough. The news of my husband's affair had already spread throughout the city. I felt like a Number One Idiot and I did not want to experience any further humiliation.

Based on the trust I had in Rachel, I went to The Healing Center for the first time. On Tuesday night, I walked into the meeting and sat on the last row. There was praise and worship and the Presence of God filled the place.

A tiny woman, Lisa, took the microphone and began to encourage everyone in increasing our faith. As I watched this little woman and the obvious anointing on her life, I began to hope, deep inside, that someday I could be as strong as she was. Hope is a beautiful thing. Don't ever stop hoping, no matter how things look!

That evening, Lisa asked, "Who is here for the first time? Please stand up and tell us your name and how you found out about The Healing Center." I stood with several others. When my turn to speak came, I said, "My name is Debra. Rachel Burchfield invited me here tonight." Everyone clapped. There was so much love in the room! Lisa walked to the back of the meeting hall and greeted me. She said, "Debra, I want to meet you. Rachel told me all about you and I have been praying for you for six weeks. I want to have lunch with you. Will you write down your phone number and I'll call you next week?" I responded eagerly, "Sure!" On the inside, I was freaking out. Why would someone like Lisa Osteen (so well known, anointed and prosperous) want to have lunch with someone like me? I was so lonely, brokenhearted, unsuccessful and financially broken.

Long story, made short, we met for lunch at a restaurant, called The Strawberry Patch, located on Westheimer Street in Houston, Texas. We instantly hit it off and became best friends.

I continued attending The Healing Center every Tuesday night. Not long after I started, I began sitting next to Lisa on the front row. I also assisted her in the meetings by doing whatever she needed. From time to time, Lisa would call me up to share a scripture or a testimony. As I look back on this time in my life, I see this was just one way God chose to help me begin restoring my dreams and placing me back into ministry. I had been crying to those closest to me, telling them I could never stand in another pulpit. I didn't believe I could ever preach the Gospel again. I was so ashamed and embarrassed about the break up of my marriage. The devil is a liar and God is faithful to put you with the right people in the right season.

When I walk down the hallway of life, I see my brother-in-law and sister, Richard and Tena Ford, who took me in on the night my husband left. They poured life into me, until I was completely healed and restored. They stuck with me and encouraged me, when I felt like everyone else had forsaken me.

They opened the door of their hearts and ministered to me, until I became the "healed" person I am today. I think about my Mom and Dad, Joe and Donnie George, (who are now in Heaven) who loved me and wrapped me in their arms during the hard times. I'd have to write another book on everything Mama and Daddy did for me. I think of Tommy and Rachel Burchfield, who dropped everything, one night, to drive out and comfort me when I was hurting. I think of my sister-in-law, Eureta George, whose nickname is Tijuana. Thank you, Tijuana, for being the one who told me I would make it, no matter what. I think of my brothers, Andrew, Johnny and Jackie, and how they believed in me. I think of Michael, Joy and Donnie Ford, who stood by me. I think of Steffie Lynn, Loveta, Annette and everyone else in my family who said, "You can make it!" I think of my friends, Linda Watson, Mark and Dena Trice, Spencer and Cyndy Nordyke and so many others who never gave up on me. God provided all of these people in my seasons of need!

And, praise God! I DID make it! YOU CAN MAKE IT TOO!! When life's hardest hits come your way, keep your head up. God's heroes are about to come on the scene. When they do, everything changes you for the better!

Key #9

Expect divine connections during the hard times.

During the lowest times of your life, God will send you to people in high places who will lift you up and out of the pit. You might be in the pit right now, but you don't have to stay there. Get up. Look up and expect to hook up with the great people that God will put along the pathway. These people are a key to your total healing. The right people, at the right time, will pull you up to another level. You're going higher, not lower. Look up!

Chapter Ten

A Prayer to Be Healed!

Before I ever started writing this book, I was praying for you. No – I may not know you personally, but because of the hatred I have for divorce, adultery and deception, I have made it one of my life's goals to pray for those who have been hurt and affected by these tragedies.

Today, I would encourage you to grab hold of the Hand of Jesus and don't let go. God has something so great in store for you! Your destiny is calling! Step into God's best for your life. Yesterday is dead! Tomorrow is not here yet! Your real life begins right now! Start living now! Don't wait around another second. Fight back!

Put your hand on your heart and pray this prayer with me out loud:

> *Father, in Jesus' Name, I pray for Your healing power to set me free.*
>
> *I thank you, that in the Name of Jesus, I can curse and destroy every tormenting thought and assignment in my life!*

> *I am making a fresh commitment to You, Jesus – to love You, to serve You, to obey You, no matter the cost!*
>
> *I'll walk with You forever, Jesus. Thank You that You are watching over me and working everything out in my favor.*
>
> *Thank You, Jesus, that I am able to step into God's dream for my life.*
>
> *My life is bright and filled with joy and peace because of You.*
>
> *Thank You for helping me step-by-step, day-by-day.*
>
> *I can walk with a spring in my step, a smile on my face and a sparkle in my eye because I know, Lord, You've got something up Your sleeve, planned just for me!*
>
> *Lord, You are good and I thank You that you're the strength of my life!*
>
> *In Jesus' Name, Amen*

Now it's time to make these bold confessions! I've made my decision. I will never quit. I will never give up. My future is so awesome. I can't stop now. I refuse to miss out on even one of the great things God has for my life!

We're not finished with our journeys, yet. Dry your eyes. Your life is not over. You are just now beginning. In fact, it's a brand new beginning for you today! Put a big smile on your face. It's time for your destiny and the beautiful plan God has for your life. It's time to discover and fulfill your God-given purpose. Come on. Let me show you how!

Key #10

Healing comes through prayer and forgiveness.

Pray each day and ask God to heal you of every past hurt. You must break the rear view mirror off of your life. Stop looking behind and, instead, look ahead. You cannot embrace your future fully, until you let go of your past.

Chapter Eleven

You Have Value

No matter what struggle you are faced with, you have to fight back! Whether you're going through depression, bankruptcy, sickness, disease, loneliness, fear or whatever, God has a great plan for your life.

Above all of God's creatures, He places a heavy-duty price tag on your life. God values you. That's why Jesus died and shed His blood on the cross. He gave His life for you. Yes, you!

You may feel like you're on the bottom. That's okay. You're on your way to the top. God's plan for your life is incredible. Allow God, not man to define your destiny.

Find your purpose! Just like God had a plan for Saul, who became the great apostle, Paul, He has a great future in mind for you. The Bible says, in Acts 26:13-19 (AMPC), "When on the road at midday, O king, I saw a light from heaven surpassing the brightness of the sun, flashing about me and those who were traveling with me. And when we had all fallen to the ground, I heard a voice in the Hebrew tongue saying to me, Saul, Saul, why do you continue to persecute Me [to harass and trouble and molest Me]? It is dangerous and turns out badly for you to keep kicking against the goads [to keep offering vain and perilous resistance]. And I said, Who are You, Lord? And the Lord said, I am Jesus, Whom you are persecuting. But arise and stand upon your feet; for I have appeared to you for this purpose, that I might appoint you to serve as [My] minister and to bear witness both to what you have seen of Me and to that in which I will appear to you, choosing you out [selecting you for Myself] and delivering you from among this [Jewish] people and the Gentiles to whom I am sending you – to open their eyes that they may turn from darkness to light and from the power of Satan to God, so that they may thus receive forgiveness and release from their sins and a place and portion among those who are consecrated and purified by faith in Me. Wherefore, O King Agrippa, I was not disobedient unto the heavenly vision."

    Just like Paul, God created you for a purpose. The Bible says, in Jeremiah 1:5 (NKJV), "Before I formed you in the womb I knew you; and before you were born I sanctified you; I ordained you a prophet to the nations." Psalm 139:14 (NKJV) says: "I will praise you, for I am fearfully and wonderfully made: marvelous are your works and that my soul knows right well."

Jesus appeared to Saul with a mission in mind. God is no respecter of persons. He has a mission in mind for you. Just like Jeremiah, God knit you together in your mother's womb. He took His time in making you. You are so special and valuable that there is no one else like you. You have great worth!

On the road to your destiny and purpose, you must change the way you think and the way you talk. In other words, you must change the way you perceive yourself. It is important for you to really like yourself. How you feel about yourself will reflect how you feel about others. The powerful scripture, Proverbs 18:21(NKJV), warns us: "Death and life are in the power of the tongue…"

Begin each day by saying the following out loud:

1. Lord, because You love me, I like myself and I realize that I am created in Your image.
2. Thank You, Lord, that You have a great future in store for me.
3. I believe my life has purpose.

4. I believe I have dignity and self-worth.

5. My future is so bright I have to wear sunglasses to stand all of the excitement!

Key #11

You are created for a great purpose.

You are not here to take up space and to breathe the air. God created you with greatness in mind. He has a special destiny that He desires for you to discover and to fulfill.

Chapter Twelve

It's Never Too Late!

The unique purpose that God has for you is so incredible! As I said before, you are not here just to take up space and breathe in oxygen. God has something so awesome planned just for you! You might be thinking you are too old or that it is too late to fulfill your purpose. That's where you're mistaken! It doesn't matter what has gone wrong in your life. God has a way of turning everything around for His glory and launching you into your God-given destiny! Here are a few things you can do to come into alignment with Him.

Keep a Grateful Attitude

The Bible says, in 1 Thessalonian 5:16-18 (AMPC), we are to "Be happy [in your faith] and rejoice and be glad-hearted continually (always); be unceasing in prayer [praying perseveringly]; thank [God] in everything [no matter what the circumstances may be, be thankful and give thanks], for this is the will of God for you [who are] in Christ Jesus [the Revealer and Mediator of that will].

Something great happens to us, on the inside, when we begin to open our mouth and thank God for all of the good things that He is doing in our lives. I have experienced the tragedy of divorce. I also understand that you may not feel like praising God and giving Him thanks. As you now know, there were so many days when I felt so numb I had a hard time thinking of things to be thankful for. But here are just a few things I make it a practice to thank Him for everyday.

- Thank Him for perfect health.
- Thank Him for a bed to sleep in.
- Thank Him for the food you eat.
- Thank Him for the clothes you wear.
- Thank Him for the family and friends you have.
- Thank Him for your job.
- Thank Him for the automobile you drive.
- Thank Him for the church you attend.
- Thank Him for the talents He has given you.
- Thank Him for the finance He provides.

- Thank Him for every good thing you have in your life.

Each day as you awake, find something to thank Him for. Thank Him that He has given you another day to fight forward and obtain all He has for your life. Whatever you are going through today, there is always someone who is going through something worse. Don't allow yourself to fall into self-pity. Keep an attitude of praise all day long. At night, before you go to sleep, tell the Lord everything and what you are grateful for. Thank Him for the smallest blessings and the larger blessings, too!

I suggest a list of at least ten I'm-thankful-for-this statements. I was told of a man who was really down. He began to write out his gratitude, just as I suggest here. It changed his life, his attitude and his outlook completely.

I'm reminded of the ten lepers in the Bible, who Jesus healed. Interestingly, only one leper turned back to thank Jesus (Luke 17:12-19). Let's emulate the one leper, mindful to turn back and give God praise for all He is doing in our lives.

The Bible clearly says, in Nehemiah 8:10, that "the joy of the Lord is our strength." It brings us joy to thank God *out loud* for His goodness and His many blessings. Everyone has something to be thankful about. You've probably heard the story of a very wealthy man who took his son to another town to stay the weekend on a farm with poor people, in hope that his son would learn to appreciate what he enjoyed daily. At the end of the trip, the father asked his son how he enjoyed the weekend. The son replied by telling his dad that he noticed quite a difference as he compared the farm and his fancy home in the city. His father was pleased and asked for further explanation. The boy replied, "I noticed that the farmer's children have six dogs and we only have one. I also noticed that we have one outside light and they have the moon and millions of stars to light up the night. And, last of all, I noticed we have a small, fenced in, yard and they have acres of pasture land to run and play in!"

In other words, no matter how much or how little you may have – instead of wishing for more, start thanking God for what you DO have! Tell God how good He is all of the time. When you praise Him, you get His attention. The Bible says He inhabits the praises of His people (Psalm 22:3). The moment you begin to thank God, you will step into your purpose. You were created to give Him praise!

Take Steps Toward Your Destination

In many instances, when you've been through a storm in life, it's so easy to lose focus and forget where you intended to go. I've heard stories about pilots, whenever they are faced with traveling through a bad storm, having to change their route. But they never change their destination. Because of your new set of circumstances, you may have to change your route, just a little, but never consider changing your destination.

Allow me to share an example of what I mean. Before my husband left me, we were youth pastors. We loved working with teenagers and, as far as I was concerned, I would have been happy to work with young people for the rest of my life. And even when my husband abruptly walked out of our marriage, my love for teens never changed. Yet, instead of continuing in my role in youth pastoring, I accepted a position, in Houston, Texas, as a second grade teacher. I needed to support myself. Deep down, I longed for the opportunity to be with teenagers again. I didn't see any way it could happen. But one day, as I was sitting and talking with my friend, Rachel Burchfield, she shared that she and her husband, Tommy, were starting a Bible school in Columbus, Texas. She went on to say that the ages of the students would range from seventeen to twenty-four years of age. I'll never forget Rachel's words, "Debra, I'm going to need your help with the school. I want you to teach." I got so excited, as I realized I was headed straight toward my destination anew. Since then, I have been teaching young people at Texas Bible Institute. On one particular day, the Lord spoke to me, saying, "You thought I had forgotten about you. Now, I'm using you to impact thousands of young graduates who will spread the Gospel all over the world."

He never forgets our destination and neither should we! Keep moving forward. Continually ask yourself where you want to go and how to get there. Ask God to assist you. He will make certain you reach your goals.

A word of caution is in order. Don't get so consumed with where you are going that you forget to enjoy the trip. Life is all about taking pleasure from our journey. I learned this lesson from my mother. Her life was not always easy. Losing a son, at a young age, in a tragic accident on the baseball field (a sport our family lived for), along with other heartaches and struggles never stopped her joy. She took the time to plant and admire flowers. She called all of her kids and encouraged them to "go outside and look at the full moon." She relished every bite of a hamburger, remarking on how it was such a treat and a blessing. She loved the television program, *Everybody Loves Raymond*, and her laughter could be heard all over the house when it aired. We all knew never to call Mama between 6:30 PM and 7 PM in the evening. We didn't interfere with Raymond. She loved him. My mother played the piano. She knew all of the old hymns, such as *The Old Rugged Cross*, but also such classics as *Five Foot Two, Eyes of Blue*. As her fingers danced over the keys, my sister, Tena, would dance! Mama wrote poems, in her spare time, and never missed a day of her Bible readings. No one ever heard her say an unkind word about anyone. Mama knew what real life was about and I am thankful she did.

The Bible says, in Psalm 37:23-24 (AMPC), that "the steps of a good man are directed and established by the Lord when He delights in his way [and He busies Himself with his every step].

Though he falls, he shall not be utterly cast down, for the Lord grasps his hand in support and upholds him." As you are taking steps toward your destination you might fall, just as the scripture says, but God will pick you up! When you fall, don't stay down. Get up again and decide you are going to press into your God-given destiny.

God knows the very number of hairs on your head. How awesome is that? He also knows how many steps you have left in life. Let me encourage you not to waste one single step. God has a way of accelerating your destiny. I'll explain through my own life example. After standing for my marriage for four years, God launched me out onto the evangelistic field. I began to travel and preach the Gospel all across the United States – and then, throughout the world.

Eventually, I began to tell the Lord how sorry I was that I had wasted so many years of my life, prior to the ministry He eventually led me to do. I felt the need to explain to Him. If I hadn't gotten into a marriage mess, I could have been out traveling and preaching all along. I felt so badly, that I had messed up God's plan for my life. But He spoke another version of my life to me.

"Debra, I'm accelerating your destiny. What would have taken twenty years to accomplish in you; I'll do in ten. Don't be sorry. Not one moment of your life has been wasted. I was developing character in you through all things." When the Lord told me this, I was elated. Suddenly, I understood God does not operate on our calendar. He has a spiritual calendar, so to speak, and what would normally take us five years to do, He can do in five months. Now, I know why I was so busy when I began to travel and preach. I was invited to speak at one meeting after another. I was away from home for weeks at a time. I know it was all because God sped up my destiny. He is ready to speed up your destiny, too. It's acceleration time for you! Get ready! God's foot is on the accelerator of your life.

    Head for your destination and don't let anyone or anything stop you! Hebrews 12:2 tells us to "look away from all that will distract to Jesus…" There will be a lot of distractions on the way. Just don't acknowledge them. Stay focused, stay alert and, by all means, take one step after another toward your goal. For every step you take, God will take one hundred and that's how you'll get to where you want to go!

Allow GOD - Not Man, to Define Your Purpose!

Man and this world will try to label you, define you, box you in and set your mold, but don't let them. If I did everything people thought I should do, over the years, I would be a crazy person by now! First of all, everyone in our family thought all individuals should get married at eighteen, have babies, babies and more babies and live happily ever after! After all, I grew up in Clodine, Texas and that's what people from Clodine do! However, God had a completely different plan for my life. Don't let anyone define your purpose. That is God's job.

No one, in my immediate family, graduated from college. That wasn't normally one of the options of the citizens of Clodine. That's why I went to work for an insurance agency, as a typist, when I graduated high school. All day long, I typed out policies. A bell would ring in the morning, which signaled a fifteen-minute break. Then, another rang for lunch and one more in the afternoon, signaling our final break of the day. After about two months, I was sick of it! I talked to my parents and they agreed to send me to college. My typist job was a drag! I wanted a job where I could talk to people, because I love to talk. I attended college and received my degree in education. The degree turned out to be the smartest thing I ever accomplished. I celebrated my first teaching job, mostly because I was *required* to talk to people all day long. That is what teaching is all about.

When I stood firm for my marriage and waited to see if my husband would return, many people disagreed with my decision. Some wanted me to forget about him and go on with my life. But deep down, I knew I was doing the right thing by standing. It's true, my husband never came home, but I can't deny the many benefits I received as a result of my course. First, the time alone caused me to draw closer to God. Second, I learned how to pray – really pray. Third, and equally as important, standing for my marriage kept me from getting involved with someone else. Fourth, it kept me from doing some other crazy thing. When I weigh the positives against the negatives, I have come out ahead by far. I know I did what God wanted me to do and that's all that really matters. Doesn't it make you feel good to know that you can be obedient to God and not man? Every night, as I lay on my pillow, I have so much peace. Do you know why?? I have no regrets. If God asked me to do it all over again, I would gladly tell

Him yes! My life is a reflection of what God can do! In the middle of your mess, God will bless you and define your purpose.

Remember when you were a child and you were told to color within the lines? Staying inside the lines was considered a school rule. Well, God's Kingdom is totally the opposite. God is looking for those who will step outside of the lines. He wants someone who is daring enough to move out of his comfort zone and do something different. Think of Peter, who was a fisherman by trade, yet dropped everything to follow to Jesus. Peter became one of the greatest soul winners known to mankind.

Think your best thoughts today! Speak your best words! Do your best! God has an awesome plan for your life. Dress for where you desire to go in the future. Keep yourself well groomed. You are a child of the most high God. You are highly favored by Him! Get ready! A big door of opportunity is right around the corner. Be ready for it!!

Stay Around Purpose Driven People

Since I started serving God, I habitually hang around with people who have purpose. Pastors Richard and Tena Ford, who brought me into the Kingdom of God and trained me, have always been people of great purpose. Just being in their presence pulled me off of the path to nowhere and put me on the street to somewhere. Your friends truly matter. God will take a nothing and turn it into something. He specializes in turning trash into treasure. He is calling you out of your shame. He is calling you by your name. That's right. You are on God's mind right now. He is thinking great thoughts about you and your future. When we remember that God sees His kids through His eyes, and not our eyes, it makes all the difference.

Just think of Daniel's friends – Shadrach, Meschach and Abednego. These three men refused to bow and worship the king's golden image. Instead, they chose to honor God. Find friends who refuse to bow to this world's standards. Stay around people with purpose, and as you build relationships with them, purpose will rub off on you.

Think about Elijah and Elisha, Moses and Joshua, Paul and Silas. The list goes on and on. Just as these people, you will become exactly like those you hang around. Maybe it's time to do a "who-do-I-hang-around?" inventory and see what you come up with. If you are the strongest, most intelligent person in your circle, it's time to shift gears. Time to move into the circle of someone who is living at your next level, or above, so you will be challenged.

I know a lady who weighed ninety-eight pounds when she married. The family she joined had a habit of staying up all hours of the night, eating pies and cakes. As a result, she began to gain weight. Before she realized completely, she was as overweight as her in-laws. She had said goodbye to her smallness by behaving like her husband's kin. She picked up their habits. It's your time to pick up good habits and leave the bad ones behind by finding those who are already living as you desire.

In the Bible, Habakkuk 1:5 (AMPC) says we should: "Look around [you, Habakkuk, replied the Lord] among the nations and see! And be astonished! Astounded! For I am putting into effect a work in your days [such] that you would not believe it if it were told you." So hold your head up high! Great days are ahead!

Key #12

It's never too late to step into your destiny!

No matter how much time you feel you've wasted, remember, nothing is ever lost with our God. He has taken all of your life experiences into consideration to form your destiny now. If things in your life have not previously been God-ordered, they will still be God-used! You can always count on Him!

Chapter Thirteen

Getting Your Stuff Back and More!

It's almost impossible to go through life and not lose something or someone. Many times, it's not what happens to us in life that counts, but *how we react* to what is happening to us that counts. I love the story about the five sisters in Numbers 27, who got all their "stuff" back and more. Let's take a look at Numbers 27:1-7 (AMPC):

1 THEN CAME the daughters of Zelophehad son of Hepher, the son of Gilead, the son of Machir, the son of Manasseh, from the families of Manasseh son of Joseph. The names of his daughters: Mahlah, Noah, Hoglah, Milcah, and Tirzah.

2 They stood before Moses, Eleazar the priest, and the leaders, and all the congregation at the door of the Tent of Meeting, saying,

3 Our father died in the wilderness. He was not among those who assembled together against the Lord in the company of Korah, but died for his own sin [as did all those who rebelled at Kadesh], and he had no sons.

4 Why should the name of our father be removed from his family because he had no son? Give to us a possession among our father's brethren.

5 Moses brought their case before the Lord.

6 And the Lord said to Moses,

7 The daughters of Zelophehad are justified and speak correctly. You shall surely give them an inheritance among their father's brethren, and you shall cause their father's inheritance to pass to them.

In this day and time, it was unheard of, and against the law, for a daughter to receive her father's inheritance after his death. The inheritance always went to the son. In this case, there was no son and these five gals decided to let their voices be heard. Not only did they get their Daddy's inheritance, but also, God spoke to Moses to change the law completely for future generations. Say it out loud, right now! "I'm going to get my stuff back and more!"

I lost so much, after my husband left. I was accustomed to having a two-salary household. Suddenly, I was down to one. I still remember how humiliated I felt, when I had to borrow $150.00 from my Dad, for a deposit on the apartment I was trying to rent. I was down so low. I had very little money and all kinds of bills to pay. I would never have considered myself as homeless, but that's how I felt, before I was able to get my apartment. I wandered from place to place, utterly depressed, and not really knowing what to do from one day to the next.

One night, I was at Eureta's (my sister-in-law) home. She couldn't help but notice how much weight I had lost, due to the trauma. It was obvious, even to me, how much she wanted me to snap out of the state of mind I was currently pursuing. I just couldn't seem to do it, at that point. I stayed another night with my niece, Natalie, and she did her best to console me. It didn't work. Night after night, house-to-house, friend-to-friend, and relative-to-relative, I roamed around, continually wondering what was going to become of me.

Slowly, but surely, things began to change. Sitting under the teachings of Pastor Richard Ford saved my life. I devoured his teachings by taking notes and, then, reading them over and over before I went to bed. I looked up every scripture he taught on. I highlighted the scriptures in my Bible and memorized many of them. The ministry of Pastor Richard Ford is a ministry full of victorious, overcoming messages. They were just what I needed. It is so important to be in the right church where faith and victory are preached. Reading Dr. James Dobson's book, titled *Love Must be Tough*, gave me strength.

Finally, I settled into my apartment. I was so lonely that I started sleeping on the side of the bed previously occupied by my husband. When my next-door neighbor tried flirting with me, I nearly knocked his head smooth off! *No thank you! I've had enough of men for a while!* I experienced all kinds of crazy emotions. One day, I was up and the next day down. I felt like I was riding a rollercoaster! Eventually, I decided to rise up and fight for what rightfully belonged to me, according to the promises of God.

I also rose up and made the decision that my life was worth living – I had value. You have to reach the place where you can pull yourself up by the bootstraps, so to speak, and move forward. I got mad – not at any particular person – but at adversity and the devil who stole from me! Just like the five daughters of Zelophehad, I decided to retrieve my inheritance. It's time for you to repeat it out loud again: "I'm going to get my stuff back and more!"

I got my dignity back! I got my self worth back! I got my joy back! I got my peace back! I got my money back! I got a good, running car! I moved into a house! I got new friends! I got opportunities!

Most importantly, I got a new relationship with a loving Jesus, who will never leave me for one moment. I lived out Joel 2:25 (AMPC): "And I will restore or replace for you the years that the locust has eaten - the hopping locust, the stripping locust and the crawling locust...." It doesn't matter who has ripped you off. Just walk away and smile. God will make everything brand new in your life. The word, "restore", means to return to its original state. Trust me, when I tell you, there are some old things that you don't want back or, perhaps, that you don't *need* back. God will give you all new stuff, if need be. It just works like that! I held onto Him and He saw to it that justice was done in my life. What God did for me, He will do for you!

Luke 13: 11-13 (AMPC) says:

11 And there was a woman there who for eighteen years had had an infirmity caused by a spirit (demon of sickness). She was bent completely forward and utterly unable to straighten herself up or to look upward.

12 And when Jesus saw her, He called [her to Him] and said to her, Woman, you are released from your infirmity!

13 Then, He laid [His] hands on her, and instantly she was made straight, and she recognized and thanked and praised God.

We don't know anything about what happened to this woman or the extent of her condition. But, think about what we **do** know. She was bent over double and unable to look her family or friends in the face. She was forced to always look at the ground. What a terrible way to live! Yet, when Jesus came on the scene, everything changed!

Invite Jesus onto the scene of your circumstances and watch Him change everything in your life, too! Reading the account of this woman's life causes me to want to encourage you to always look up. Never look down! He's the glory and the lifter of your head! Jesus always lifts us up. He will never put us down. When Satan has us bound, Jesus makes us free! In fact, Jesus will break all the rules of man's traditions, just to touch you! In Biblical times, only men were allowed to come into where Jesus called for this little bent-over woman!

Today, Jesus is calling you to come to Him, so He can heal your mind and body, restore your family and your finances. He wants to grab hold of your sons and daughters. Do not sit back passively and let life pass you by. It's time for you to rise up and see God move in a new and fresh way!

Key #13

Believe you will get back everything you've lost and more!

As I mentioned earlier, some of the old things (and possibly even old relationships) may have to go. God has brand new things and relationships He desires to freely give you. When life's circumstances are weighing you down and have you "bent", like the woman in Luke 13, know this: God will straighten it all out for you, just like he straightened out the woman's body!

Chapter Fourteen

Be a Prisoner of Hope

Zechariah 9:12 (AMPC) says the following: "Return to the stronghold [of security and prosperity], you prisoners of hope; even today do I declare that I will restore double your former prosperity to you." Notice the word, "today". Not tomorrow, not someday, but today! We serve a today God. A right now God!

Let's look at Isaiah 43:18-19 (AMPC):

18 Do not [earnestly] remember the former things; neither consider the things of old.
19 Behold, I am doing a new thing! Now it springs forth; do you not perceive and know it and will you not give heed to it? I will even make a way in the wilderness and rivers in the desert."
Notice the word, "now." God wants to do something great in your life right now, but you must become a prisoner of hope.

There are many times that we allow wrong, negative thoughts to live in our mind "rent free." But no more! Today is the day you must decide to change the way you think about things. God wants to do something new in your life. He wants to give you new thoughts. If there were one single thing I feel the need to advise you about, it would be to change the way you contemplate! The only way you will be able to accomplish this goal is to change what you're looking at and what you're seeing. It is proven fact that your life moves in the direction of your strongest, most predominant thought. What are you meditating on? Change your thinking and you'll change your direction. Change your direction and you'll change your whole life!

You've seen my response. When I was going through my own difficult time, I read my Bible continually - even on my breaks at work! I knew I had to replace my old negative thought patterns. Those silent messages playing in my head that kept repeating, "You'll never amount to anything or you'll never make it." I worked hard to substitute positive statements such as: " I will amount to someone great! I will be an overcomer in every circumstance that life brings me!" You may be thinking, *"Debra, that is very easy for you to say. You're on the other side of your pain, while I am right in the middle of my storm."* If you are standing directly inside your trial, then listen up! It takes the same amount of energy to think positive, as it does to think negative. Rise up! Get your boxing gloves on! It's time to get your hopes up! Your situation is about to catch up to your revelation! When it does, look out! The sky is the limit! Keep your mind filled with thoughts of hope and success.

To be a prisoner of hope, you must forget the past! Break your symbolic rearview mirror off of the car and throw it away! Stop looking behind you and start looking in front of you. Jesus says, in Luke 9:62 (NKJV), that "no man having put his hand to the plow, and looking back is fit for the kingdom of God." Jesus understood the importance of not looking back. Unfortunately, life is not a dress rehearsal. We only go through this life one time. We can't go back and change anything. That's why it's called life. It's a journey through which we only learn by making mistakes. Stop the habit, right now, of putting yourself down. Never view yourself as a failure. See yourself as a learner!

Live your life as if you believe what you are saying to yourself. I'm reminded of the woman, in the Bible, who couldn't stop bleeding. Mark 5:28 (AMPC) tells us how she kept saying, "If I only touch His garments, I shall be restored to health." Notice how she "kept saying." She didn't say it once, and when it didn't happen, give up. No. She kept saying what she believed. I don't believe those are the only words she said to herself (or even out loud). I think she also kept saying, "The pain is gone. The bleeding has stopped. No more expensive doctor bills." She lived like she believed indeed! She also received what she believed and you will too!

We must believe that God will give us double for our trouble. Life and its trials have a way of pulling us down! Sometimes, without even knowing it, we bring trouble upon ourselves. You may have broken dreams and be living inside despair. Try to look at your situation this way. When something goes wrong, thank God you've just been put in a position to receive double for your trouble. In other words, God considers all of the injustices that have occurred in your life, then takes out his Heavenly calculator, adds them up and hands you a double portion of blessings in return! Consider Micah 7:8 (AMPC), written to reassure us: "Rejoice not against me, O my enemy! When I fall I shall arise; when I sit in darkness, the Lord shall be a light to me." It's your time to arise. We may be products of our past, but we don't have to be prisoners of our past.

Remember, your walk follows your talk. Proverbs 6:2 (AMPC) says, " You are snared with the words of your lips, you are caught by the speech of your mouth." Proverbs 18:21 lets us know that, "Death and life are in the power of the tongue." Stop saying things like: "My kids are bad kids." or "I'll never have any money." Change your world by changing your words. We've learned how to train our children and our dogs. And, now, we need to retrain our tongues. Rephrase your words. "I have the best children in the world." After all, you had them! Honestly, you make yourself look bad when you speak negatively about them.

Lastly, live with favor on your mind. The Bible tells us, in Psalm 5:12, that "His favor surrounds us with a shield..." To be surrounded means we are all encompassed with his favor, much like surround sound from a television or stereo unit. Favor is everywhere you go. When people see you, they will automatically want to be nice to you. They will want to be good to you. That's what favor is. I think of Rahab, the prostitute, and how she found favor with the spies, because she hid them in her home from their enemies (read Joshua, Chapter 2). Because of favor, the lives of Rahab's entire family were spared. On top of that, Rahab left her old lifestyle behind and married a man of God. She ended up listed in the lineage of Jesus. That's favor. God's unprecedented favor is on your life as well. Before you even reach out to turn off your alarm clock each morning, start thinking about favor. Say things like: "I have the favor of God on my life! I am highly favored today!"

Don't be a prisoner of hopelessness. Rise up. Choose to be a prisoner of hope. Trap yourself firmly inside hope. Don't lie down and allow your circumstances to conquer you. Get up and conquer with your faith and His favor!

Key #14

Hope is the beginning of your complete healing and breakthrough. Get your hopes up!

Don't focus on the way things are now. Focus on where your faith in God is taking you. Work on envisioning your future. You are the only one who can see this picture. It is sitting there inside your spirit. Look past where you are now to where God intends you to go. Once you get a firm picture in your spirit, you're almost there. God will honor your hope and faith!

Chapter Fifteen

Follow Your Passions

We never have to doubt God has a future for us. Jeremiah 29:11 (MSG) shows us God's intentions, "I know what I'm doing, I have it all planned out; plans to take care of you, not abandon you, plans to give you the future you hope for." And Paul, in his letter to Philippi (Philippians 3:13 AMPC), gives us our attitude adjustment. "I do not consider, brethren, that I have captured and made it my own [yet]; but one thing I do [it is my one aspiration]; forgetting what lies behind and straining forward to what lies ahead, I press on toward the goal to win the [supreme and heavenly] prize to which God in Christ Jesus is calling us upward."

God created you to be full of life. He desires for you to be passionate, excited, joyful, upbeat, energetic, happy, positive and enthusiastic! Too often, when the trials and storms of life come along, we get sidetracked. Instead of being excited about our future, we get bored, unenthusiastic, empty and just start going through the motions. It's time for you to get excited about your future! It's time for you to follow your passions. Let me show you how.

Let's start with Ephesians 2:10 (AMPC), which says: "For we are God's [own] handiwork (His workmanship), recreated in Christ Jesus, [born anew] that we may do those good works which God predestined (planned beforehand) for us [taking paths which He prepared ahead of time], that we should walk in them [living the good life which He prearranged and made ready for us to live]."

Next, let's read Jeremiah 1:5 (AMPC): "Before I formed you in the womb I knew [and] approved of you [as My chosen instrument], and before you were born I separated and set you apart, consecrating you; [and] I appointed you as a prophet to the nations."

God already approves of you. He loves you just like you are, but He loves you too much to leave you the way you are. He desires for you to be passionate about life. It's sad to say that one of the richest places on earth is probably a graveyard. Graveyards are full of dreams that were never birthed, businesses that were never started, songs that were never sung, books that were never written, inventions that never came to fruition, and ministries that were never started. Why? Because these buried individuals never took the time to identify their passions and follow them.

Remember how I told you I quit working at an insurance company and chose to become a school teacher instead? I quit typing policies because I wasn't passionate about the job. I didn't enjoy doing it. I love working with people. I am passionate about helping people achieve their life destinies and becoming all God wants them to be. Fulfillment comes when we follow our passions. It's just as important to know what we are NOT passionate about, as it is to know what we love doing. Some folks spend their entire lives going to jobs every day that they actually hate. And they wonder, all along, why they are not fulfilled.

Passion is something that burns on the inside of you! It's the thing that wakes you up in the morning. It's the last thing you think about and pray about before you go to sleep each night. My greatest passion is winning souls for Jesus. I'm also passionate about seeing sick bodies healed. I love preaching the Gospel of Jesus Christ! If you took these things away from me, I would feel useless.

Following your true passion means you will have to pay a price. I've paid to get where I'm at today. It cost me something. In fact, it cost me everything! Today, I live a life totally surrendered to the Holy Spirit. I'm committed to performing the will of God in my life. I didn't get to this place overnight. I had a lot of dying to self to do. Dying to my own flesh and my own plans, before I gravitated to the place of utter surrender to Him. What many people do not know is after my divorce was final and the Lord had spoken to me and told me to travel and preach His Good News, I did not actually want to go. In fact, I informed God of my plans, "I'm not going!" He responded, "Yes, you are!" Needless to say He won! But, the point is, the Lord and I spent many sleepless nights fighting over whether or not I would follow His will or my will. Somewhere inside the struggle, I finally gave up and said, " Dear Jesus, if You can use someone like me, I'll go, but I'm asking You to anoint me when I open my mouth." Since that moment, even until now, God has anointed the words that have come out of my mouth. I still am, and will always be, humbled about how God can use such an ordinary person. Yet, if I had to go through the struggle all over again, I would gladly do it again in order to have more of Jesus and much, much less of Debra.

We've all heard many teachings about how Jacob wouldn't let go of the angel until God blessed him (Genesis 32:26). But, I like to say that God wouldn't let go of Jacob until He changed him. God wants us to change, my friend. He will go to any length to get you and me to the place of total surrender.

Stirring Up the Passion Around Our Desires

What are your personal desires? What is burning on the inside of you? Is it a marriage that you want to see restored? Is it a business that you know you should start? Ask yourself right now. And then, tell God about them. Make a list to help you remember. Examples: "I desire to be a better Christian. I desire to win souls. I desire to be blessed financially, so that I can help others. I desire…..anything else." Begin to speak your desires out loud, so that you can hear them. Come on! It's not time for you to pick out your tombstone, so get busy living!

The poorest person in the world is not actually a person who doesn't have any money. The poorest person in the world is the one who does not have any passion. Desires have a way of growing within, until you are so pregnant with them, you have no choice but to give birth!

Let's study up on the subject:

In the Bible, Mark 11:24 (AMPC) instructs us to ask, "For this reason I am telling you, whatever you ask for in prayer believe (trust and be confident) that it is granted to you, and you will [get it]."

In Proverbs 29:18 (AMPC), we are given a warning, "Where there is no vision [no redemptive revelation of God], the people perish; but he who keeps the law [of God, which includes that of man] – blessed (happy, fortunate, and enviable) is he."

When you have no picture of your future, you become discouraged. Notice the word "desire" in Mark 11:24. Your desire is directly tied to your destiny. Don't just pray for what you need. Pray about your desires. What you desire holds your destiny.

I love to use my Daddy as an example. Before he went home, to be with the Lord at the age of 91, Daddy loved to coon hunt. Now, unless you're from Clodine, Texas, you may not know what coon hunting is all about. My Dad traveled all over Texas, just to find the best dogs to hunt raccoon. Our coon dogs were named, Bell, Hobo and Maggy. When I was a young girl, I would go inside the dog pen, during the week, and try to get them to play with me. Those ole' dogs were so lazy. All they wanted to do was lay around and sleep. I would tug on their ears, pull on their fur, pull their tails, and still, they would refuse to play. Maggy was so picky about her dog food that Mama would have to cook a special gravy on her stove to pour over her food, in order to entice her to eat. These dogs were definitely not my idea of fun!

Still, when Friday night rolled around and my Dad cranked up his pickup truck, the dogs came alive. They jumped up, barked and ran to the gate. All you had to do was lift the latch and they ran straight to the back of Daddy's truck. They were all fired up and ready to go tree a coon! Maggy might have a whole pan of her special gravy sitting in the pen, but she would run right past it just to go hunting. You see, these dogs were doing what they were born to do. They were living out their passion of coon hunting.

There is something you were born to do. Once you discover what it is, you'll never be satisfied doing anything else. In fact, just like Maggy, you'll even run past things you ordinarily like, to do the thing you love. Don't allow the enemy of God's best, called "good", to distract you. Stir up your passions. Stir up your spiritual desires. An incredible destiny is waiting for you!

Be Enthusiastic!

I love what the Bible says in Romans 12:11 (AMPC): "Never lag in zeal and in earnest endeavor; be aglow and burning with the Spirit, serving the Lord." Be enthusiastic about each day. Enjoy where you are, on the way to where you're going. Remember, life is not just about your destination. It's more about your journey. So, choose to enjoy today. Don't say, "I'll be happy when I have more money." Or, "I'll be happy when my children are grown." No, don't ever say, " I'll be happy when…" God wants to know you are choosing to be happy right now!

It's important to realize Satan is not after you. Don't take his attacks personally. He's after your enthusiasm. He's after your desire. He's after your dreams. Why? If he can get you to stop dreaming and never be enthusiastic, then he's accomplished his purpose of causing you to take your eyes off of the plan God has for your life! Don't let him win! Be enthusiastic, happy and upbeat about everyday life. The Bible also says, in Proverbs 17:22

(NKJV), "A merry heart does good, like medicine." Learn to laugh. The more you laugh, the better you will feel. This fact has actually been proven medically. Even if you have to watch old reruns of your favorite sitcom, do whatever it takes to get your enthusiasm back!

Create a Bigger Vision for Your Life

Isaiah 54:2-3 (AMPC) lets us know about how to create a life of vision: "Enlarge the place of your tent, and let the curtains of your habitations be stretched out; spare not; lengthen your cords and strengthen your stakes, for you will spread abroad to the right hand and to the left; and your offspring will possess the nations and make the desolate cities to be inhabited."

Use your faith! Remember the story of the twelve spies that went to check out the land? The spies returned and spoke of giants and how they considered themselves as small as grasshoppers in the giant's sight. However, Joshua and Caleb returned with a great report, saying it was time for them to go in and possess the land (see Numbers 13). Allow me to ask you a question. Do you see yourself as a giant or as a grasshopper? In other words, it's time for you to think bigger. Talk big. Walk big. Act big. You serve a BIG

God. Get rid of your grasshopper mentality. Enlarge the picture of your future. Whatever you're thinking of today, or dreaming of for your future, think bigger. Ephesians 3:20 (AMPC) speaks to us, "Now to Him Who, by (in consequence of) the [action of His] power that is at work within us, is able to [carry out His purpose and] do superabundantly, far over and above all that we [dare] ask or think [infinitely beyond our highest prayers, desires, thoughts, hopes or dreams]."

Think bigger. Think greater. Why should you believe for something small when you serve such a big God? Nothing big ever comes out of thinking small.

Trust God for His Perfect Timing

Ecclesiastes 3:1 (AMPC) let us know, "TO EVERYTHING there is a season, and a time for every matter or purpose under heaven." No one, but God, can understand His timing. I can tell you this: God is never, ever late. He will always be exactly on time. Just when you think things are not working out, God is faithful and He will come through for you every time you need Him to come through. The key is never, ever give up! Anyone can quit! Don't you ever be one of those people; don't quit! Stay in the race of life! You'll never know about the great things God has for you, unless you keep pressing forward! Run to win and you will!

Key #15

**Whatever burns inside your heart is a desire!
Those desires are connected to your destiny!**

Pay attention to your desires. Almighty God placed them within you. When you listen to them, you will be placing yourself right in the center of His perfect will! I learned, on my journey, to follow my passions, to stay close to them. Give your undivided attention to whatever puts a bounce in your step and smile on your face. Don't fall into the trap of going to a job, day after day, that you absolutely despise. Trust God for the way you can step into your purpose. Trust also that He will bring you any necessary provision. God created you for His purpose. Your belief in Him should enable you to take a teeny tiny step today towards your destiny. He will guide you through to your destination.

Chapter Sixteen

Wake Up Your Dream!

Deep inside you there is a dream from Almighty God. His dream has been nestled in you before you were even born. Jeremiah 1:5 talks of how God knew and approved of Jeremiah before he was in his mother's womb. The same is true for you. God even ordained Jeremiah to be a prophet at that time! Wow!

We serve a God who is sovereign. As I said earlier, we were not put on this earth to take up space and merely breathe in oxygen. God has a reason for your being here. I believe, from the time I was born, God ordained that I would be a soul winner. To be a soul winner, one shares Jesus Christ with others in order to move them from Hell to Heaven.

One day, we will all stand before God and the decision to live for Jesus Christ must be made on this earth. Some years back, I stepped into my God-given destiny and began to win souls. My life was profoundly touched and changed by my own sister, Tena, who led me to Jesus Christ, in the living room of her home, when I was twenty years old. In her home, I was saved, filled with the Holy Ghost and set on fire for Jesus Christ.

There were many times when I was with my sister that I saw, firsthand, the boldness of Jesus in operation. She shared her faith in Christ wherever she was and led many to Him. She's still doing this today. To see such a great soul winner in action forever marked me to try also to make a difference in my own world.

When I was preaching, at a church in Mobile, Alabama, I stayed in the home of a friend, named Carolyn Dyson. That night, I couldn't sleep and picked up a book from her shelf, titled, *This Is That*, by Aimee Semple McPherson. Ms. McPherson was a great soul winner. She resides in Heaven today. When I began to read the accounts of all of the souls she led to Jesus, I began to weep uncontrollably. I didn't understand exactly what was happening to me then, but now I know God was waking up His dream on the inside of me to win people to Jesus Christ.

After I returned home from Alabama, I was sitting in my one-bedroom, decorated in pink, apartment when Jesus visited me. Deep down inside my spirit, He spoke to me, saying, "Debra, I've called you to be a soul winner and from this day forward the anointing on your life to win souls will intensify." This visitation from Jesus forever changed the course of my life. Less than twenty-four hours later, I found myself standing in a dark alley on the outskirts of Houston, Texas, preaching Jesus Christ to about sixteen teenagers and one mother. All of them accepted Christ that night and were gloriously born again. From that moment forward, everywhere I went, I was leading people to Jesus.

Even after having these great revelations, and after a bit of time passed, I realized I wasn't leading people to Christ like I had originally. Many of us can freely admit life happens. What I mean is, sometimes, we get so busy doing so many different things, we lose sight of our dreams. This is exactly what happened to me. In my particular "life happens" moment, my father became ill and spent the last several months of his life going back and forth to the hospital. I was spending a lot of time with my Mom, as well, making sure she was okay. When my Dad went home to be with the Lord in 2005, I spent more and more time at my Mother's house. I felt like I needed to keep her company. Truthfully, she kept me company too, and we had two more glorious years together, before the angels of God swept Mama away to behold Jesus face to face.

Daddy was gone. Mama was gone. You, too, may have experienced your own circumstances similar to mine. In the midst of our busy lives, there are moments when we just don't realize our fire for God is dwindling. Our dream for God is not gone – just asleep.

I meet so many people, like me, every day. They have a dream from God, but somehow, it got put on the bottom shelf. There it can be forgotten, if we do not wake it up. We can live and die and never fulfill our God-given destiny. I don't want that to happen to you, my friend, and this is precisely why I have taken this last chapter to talk to you about how God woke up my dream and He is longing to wake yours up too!

I recognized I needed to wake my dream back up and I went on an all out search. By this, I mean I went to special meetings, read every book I could get my hands on, watched on fire preachers on television and, then, one day it happened.

I saw two women of God winning souls in the inner city. They were also preaching the Gospel of Jesus Christ all over the world. When I laid eyes on them, I thought to myself, *"They are living their dreams! I'm going to live mine too!"* I began to grab hold of my destiny. I began to sow into the ministries of these two special ladies. In order to wake up our own dream, we must first be willing to sow into someone else's dream. So, that's what I did. I prayed God would divinely connect me to these women for His purposes. He answered my prayer.

On many evenings, I got up off of my sofa and kneeled in front of my television as one or the other was preaching. I asked God to give me favor with them. They didn't even know who I was, but God knew us all. He opened the door and released a greater soul winning anointing on my life than I have ever dreamed would be possible. I wanted to win even more souls. God connected me with women who were winning more souls than I could at the time. You'll probably be able to guess what happened next. I fell into sync with those very women, winning more souls over to Him than ever. My dream had come alive!

I met a crack addict/hooker and led her to Jesus. She, in turn, introduced me to the drug infested neighborhood where she lived. She and I, along with a group of my friends, visited this area, winning soul after soul. To this day, everywhere I go, I'm winning souls and training other soul winners across the world. I'm living my dream. I'm living my destiny.

What Jesus has done for me, He can and will do for you! All we have to do is follow His plan to wake up our dreams. Remember, though, life is not only about your destination. It's also about your journey, including the people you will meet along the way. These people have the potential to change your life forever. During my journey, I received both spiritual growth and wisdom from Pastors Richard and Tena Ford. Richard and Tena were the first people to believe in me. They were the first to give me the opportunity to preach in their pulpit. Wow! We need to thank God for people, like them, who will trust us and open up opportunities for us to grow!

Pastors Tommy and Rachel Burchfield, my lifelong friends, have extended such favor toward me throughout the years. They have opened doors for me everywhere, allowing me to teach in their Bible school (Texas Bible Institute, Columbus, Texas).

Two additional women, Darlene Bishop and Paula White, intersected my life and threw some fuel on my God-given dream when I needed it most.

The same God who gave me the desires of my heart will give you the desires of your heart. My dream from God stayed inside me all of those years. It had only been covered up by the trials of life. This can easily happen to anyone at one time or another.

Here's your mission for today. Get in the vicinity of someone who is doing what you desire to do. Let someone who is living his/her dream wake yours up. I declare, right now, your best days are right in front of you. In fact, your best days are right now! You are stepping into your God-given destiny. Don't ever stop chasing it. Don't ever quit. Don't ever look back. No time in our lives has been wasted. Today is the greatest day of the rest of your life. You have been chosen by Almighty God to do something great with your life on this earth. You are a son or daughter of destiny. Throw your shoulders back! Put a big smile on your face. Life happens to all of us. It's how we respond to what occurs that means everything. Our best response is connecting with God and pouring out our hearts and souls to Him.

He is listening to our prayers always. He is hearing our voices, no doubt, and is ready to give us the desires of our hearts. So, stop living with a dream that is asleep. Tell your dream to wake up right now! Get up and run after it with everything in you! I promise this. You will never regret pursuing the dreams and desires God has placed inside of you. When you run after your dream, like I did, you'll be able to stand at the end of your life and say, "My God, the dream is indeed true and I'm so glad I decided to fulfill my purpose in life!"

Nothing can keep you down or defeat you when you serve Jesus Christ. Grab the Word of God and refuse to let go. His promises will surely come to pass. You are too valuable to Him to quit now. Hurt always stops when we walk with Jesus and believe His plan for our lives are so much greater than we can ever imagine. You are a person of great worth. You are valuable to Jesus and to this world. Press forward through every obstacle. Get close to Him. When you do, you will be a champion in life no matter what!

Key#16

God has placed His dreams inside you
and intends that they come to pass!

God is not a tease. He doesn't promise something and not let you have it. Stay in hot pursuit of your dreams. Bathe your dreams in prayer. Speak God's Word over your life and watch God move on your behalf. Believe God will connect you to the right people to help you along. Shout it out loud: "God, wake up Your dream living inside me in the Name of Jesus!" Now go! Run! Chase! You're on a journey where all things are possible!

About the Author

Hands down, people everywhere refer to Debra as being a winner of souls. Pastor Lisa Osteen Comes, Debra's best friend for over twenty years, refers to her as one of the greatest soul winners she has had the privilege to know, other than her own father, Pastor John Osteen of Lakewood Church. Pastor Paula White says Debra is a "soul winner's soul winner" and a "preacher's preacher" who is raising up an army for Jesus across the world.

Debra describes herself simply: "I'm a girl from Clodine, Texas - farmer's daughter, raised around a bunch of crazy people. Being the youngest of six children, we loved a lot, laughed a lot and danced a lot to Motown. We also played lots and lots of baseball in our yard or the cow pasture. Our bases were either trees or old catalogs they sent to Mama. We often made up our own rules, but funny enough, one of my brothers, Johnny Joe George, caught the attention of some baseball scouts and ended up playing pro! We were so proud of him.

My life has been shaped by my parents, Joe and Donnie George, who always had the ability to touch hurting humanity, whether it was the men (who were, at that time, referred to as bums) who jumped off the freight trains in front of Mama's house to get a good meal or someone who needed money or those who required a ride to the hospital in the middle of the night. My folks loved and helped everybody!

When I was twenty, my sister, Tena, led me to Christ during College Spring Break. That was the day I gave my life to Jesus and started serving Him with everything in me. My greatest joy is to pass on the message that no matter who you are or what you've done, you are greatly loved and valued by our God! It is my personal privilege to love God, love people, help them and preach the Gospel of Jesus Christ across the world.

Thank you for reading, *When Hurt Won't Stop*. I believe whatever season of your life you are currently living inside, this book will encourage you, strengthen you, inspire you and heal you.

Made in the USA
Columbia, SC
13 April 2019